NEUROMARKETING

Understanding the "Buy Button" in Your Customer's Brain

Patrick Renvoisé and Christophe Morin

THOMAS NELSON
Since 1798

NASHVILLE DALLAS MEXICO CITY RIO DE JANEIRO BEIJING

Published in Nashville, Tennessee, by Thomas Nelson. Thomas Nelson is a trademark
of Thomas Nelson, Inc.

Thomas Nelson, Inc., titles may be purchased in bulk for educational,
business, fundraising, or sales promotional use. For information, please
e-mail SpecialMarkets@ThomasNelson.com.

© Custom Photos by Frederic Neema of Frederic Neema Photography
www.fnphoto.com

Library of Congress Cataloging-in-Publication Data

Renvoisé, Patrick.
   Neuromarketing : understanding the "buy button" in your customer's brain / Patrick
Renvoisé and Christophe Morin. -- Rev. and updated.
        p. cm.
   Rev. ed. of the English ed. with title: Neuromarketing. 2002-2005.
   An earlier English ed. also published with title: Selling to the old brain. 2002-2003.
   ISBN 978-0-7852-2680-2
   ISBN 978-1-59555-135-1 (IE)
1. Neuromarketing. 2. Marketing--Psychological aspects. 3. Consumers' preferences.
4. Neuropsychology. I. Morin, Christophe. II. Title.
   HF5415.12615.R46 2007
   658.8001'9--dc22

                                                                    2007029695

Printed in the United States of America
07 08 09 10 QWM   2 3 4 5 6

*To my wife, Nathalie, for her unconditional support
during the long and lonely months of research work
that led to this book. Her love is a constant source of energy.*

*To our son Theo. At the tender age of 4
he already knew how to push our "Buy Button"!*

~Patrick Renvoisé

*To Bonnie for her support, love, and for giving me
the strength to be true to myself and my passion.*

*To my sons Elliott and Oliver, hoping that they will use principles
of this book to increase their future success and happiness.*

~Christophe Morin

CONTENTS

FOREWORD

Dear Reader,

Within your cranium lies the most evolved object in the known universe—the human brain.

This small organ of 1,500 cubic centimeters and 6 kilograms contains over 100 billion living cells and 1 million kilometers of interconnecting fiber. What is more, it only requires the power level of a 60-watt incandescent light bulb to operate—the equivalent of three meals a day!

But exactly how does it function? How do we derive our emotions, our motivations, and our decisions, big and small, from such a compact and complex device?

In this book Patrick and Christophe bring forth a new theory that explains how the brain arrives at its conclusions—both consciously and subconsciously—and when this happens automatically and independently of our educated logic.

Step by step we are led to understand the interaction between the "old brain" and the "new brain," and how the former overrides the latter in matters ranging from survival to everyday decision making. The conclusion: twenty-first-century educated consumers have less control over their rational choices and decisions than they may think!

As the book reveals, our old brain, the "reptilian brain," has retained a remarkable grip over our everyday lives, in spite of the enlarged "neo-cortex," the new brain, that has evolved to wrap around it physically. Yet it is indeed the neo-cortex which distinguishes human beings from all other primates on our planet. In spite of our modern ability to analyze and rationalize complex scenarios and situations, the old brain will regularly override all aspects of this analysis and, quite simply, veto the new brain's conclusions.

The interaction between the old brain and the new brain is exactly the thesis of this book—an interaction that sheds light on the new phrase "neuromarketing." Such areas as public speaking, presentation making, proposal writing, consulting, and many other dimensions of sales and marketing are all subject to such interactions. More specifically, the book identifies the language of the old brain versus the language of the new brain, and how we can speak to each accordingly.

Sales and marketing professionals at all levels will learn how to diagnose the underlying pain that clients are dealing with and how to recognize the hidden elements of financial, strategic, and personal pain contained therein. And of equal importance, the reader will learn the critical aspects of building trust and credibility with clients in today's dynamic world—a world of fast-moving claims and counter-claims where deeper human relationships are often sadly overlooked.

Individuals on both sides of the equation—buyers and suppliers—will each benefit from a thorough knowledge of the principles contained in *Neuromarketing: Understanding the "Buy Button" in Your Customer's Brain*. The book reveals what our most admired professionals know intuitively.

This is a wonderful read that will influence your business as well as your daily affairs. Neuromarketing is opening a new era where the art of influencing is being enhanced by science.

Bob Bishop

Chairman and Founder,
BBWORLD Consulting Services
Geneva, Switzerland.

Chairman, Strategic Advisory Board,
EPFL Blue Brain Project
Lausanne, Switzerland.

Former Chairman and CEO,
Silicon Graphics, Inc.
Mountain View, California.

PREFACE

In 2002, during twelve months of retreat and extensive research in sales, marketing, and neuroscience, I developed the basis of a method called Selling to Old Brain, now recognized as the first Neuromarketing model.

I shared my work with a few friends, all sales and marketing professionals, including Christophe Morin the then-Chief Marketing officer at RStar—a publicly traded company. Christophe's feedback was similar to my other friends' who all gave great positive feedback to the draft of the book... but I couldn't trust any of them. As friends it was predictable that their opinions would support of my work.

However, Christophe went further: he volunteered to edit the book, quit his job, and co-founded SalesBrain, a company which would be dedicated to applying the principle of that method.

For an additional twelve months, Christophe and I partnered to refine the book and present a solid, proven formula to increase anyone's selling effectiveness. The book is still narrated by me, Patrick, as when I produced the first draft. You'll find it packed with stories, examples, and an effective, scientific formula for success. Today this book is available in seven languages, and over 10,000 sales and marketing professionals have been exposed to the method.

May the power of the Old Brain be with you!

Patrick Renvoisé

INTRODUCTION

Have you ever been in a sales situation where you were absolutely convinced you had the best solution for your prospect, but you still lost the deal? Even the best of us have experienced this paradox.

Selling today is tougher than ever because:

- Buyers are more sophisticated, and they are inundated with information.
- Competition is more intense.
- Sales cycles are longer.
- Buying by committee is more common.
- Resistance to traditional closing techniques has increased.

Fortunately, learning about neuromarketing will quickly increase your selling effectiveness, enabling you to push your customers' "Buy Buttons" and rapidly:

- Deliver convincing sales presentations.
- Shorten your sales cycle.
- Close more deals.
- Create effective marketing strategies.
- Boost your revenue and profits.
- Radically improve your ability to influence others.

You will also learn how to craft compelling messages in your marketing material and on your Web site that will bring you a constant flow of new prospects. These techniques can even be used to raise money for your business or to gain new jobs or promotions.

Before we enter into the science of the old brain, let me tell you a short story about how I made $960 an hour consulting for a homeless man. Here is how it happened:

One evening, as I was entering a restaurant in San Francisco, a homeless person stopped me. He was displaying an all-too-common cardboard sign that said: "Homeless. PLEASE HELP."

The man showed all the signs of distress, and his eyes held a sad emptiness—a poor fellow indeed. I do not pretend to be an altruist, but often when a poor person looks me directly in the eyes, my conscience demands that I hand over a dollar or two. On this occasion, I went one step further than giving him a dollar: I decided to increase his selling effectiveness—"It's better to teach a man to fish than to give him a fish."

The first challenge my would-be client faced was the same that many individuals or companies face: his message was weak, and certainly not unique. There are thousands of homeless people in San Francisco, and they are all asking for "help." So I handed over two dollars under one condition: that he would let me change the message on his cardboard sign for at least two hours. I even promised him an additional five dollars if he was still there when I came out of the restaurant. Even if he thought my message wouldn't work, I wanted to give him incentive to try.

The man agreed, so I picked up his cardboard sign, wrote a new message on the reverse side, and walked inside the restaurant with my friends. Two hours later, we met the man again on our way out. He refused to take my five dollars. Instead, the homeless man insisted on giving me ten! He happily told me how he had made sixty dollars in the two hours that I was eating dinner.

Since his typical "take" averaged between two and ten dollars an hour, the man was truly thankful. He forced me to accept his ten dollars. As the entire interaction had lasted only thirty seconds, this eight-dollar profit translates into $960 an hour.

What did his new cardboard sign say? "What if YOU were hungry?"

I did not realize at the time why this message had unparalleled impact. It spoke a powerful language understood by the true decision-maker, a language that has the power to change sales and marketing principles forever.

True, there is no shortage of books on the field of sales and marketing. So why write another one? Throughout our careers, Christophe and I have read a great number of sales and marketing books and attended every major training program on the market. Yet at the end of each new book or program, our selling effectiveness had increased by only a few points at best. We came to realize that although sales and marketing material may be extensive, none of it utilizes the latest findings in neuroscience to teach how people make buying decisions!

While current books and training programs focus primarily on tactical issues relating to topics such as lead generation, prospect qualification, funnel management, and decision-maker identification, this book introduces you to a completely new language to build and deliver messages that influence the true decision-maker—the old brain. The language of the old brain is not only simple and easy to remember, it also offers a unique communication platform that dramatically increases your selling effectiveness, allowing you to reach a sustained higher level of success in all your sales, marketing, and communication efforts.

I am now happy to share with you the science that has revolutionized the best way to sell. But first, a disclaimer: when neuromarketing first emerged as a promising new branch in the tree of marketing disciplines, some considered it a threatening and manipulative technique.

In fact it is the opposite.

I believe that unraveling the decision-making mechanism in the brain helps you become aware of your own decision-making patterns. This in effect will help you assess if people are trying to manipulate you or if they are simply trying to influence you for your own benefit.

By the end of this book, I expect you will agree.

THREE BRAINS, ONE DECISION-MAKER

Brain: an apparatus with which we think we think.
~AMBROSE BIERCE, AUTHOR

Having the best technology or the highest quality solution does not guarantee that prospects will always buy from you. But exciting new findings in brain research suggest that speaking to the true decision-maker, the old brain, will raise your effectiveness in communicating an idea or selling a product.

You probably already know the distinction often made between the left brain and the right brain. The left hemisphere is the center of linear thinking such as language, logic, and mathematics. The right hemisphere is the center of conceptual thoughts such as art, music, creativity, and inspiration.

The brain can also be categorized into three distinct parts that act as separate organs with different cellular structures and different functions. Although these three parts of the brain communicate with each other and constantly try to influence each other, each one has a specialized function:

- *The new brain* **thinks.** It processes rational data.
- *The middle brain* **feels.** It processes emotions and gut feelings.
- *The old brain* **decides.** It takes into account the input from the other two brains, but the old brain is the actual trigger of decision.

The old brain is a primitive organ, a direct result of the basic evolutionary process. It is our "fight or flight" brain—our survival brain—and is also called the reptilian brain because it is still present in reptiles today. In fact, any animal with vertebrae has a spine within its vertebrae, and the top end of that spine is 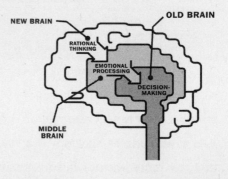 indeed the old brain. Some people call the old brain the "first brain," as it appeared first—before we grew a middle brain and a new brain. Furthermore, while our brains grow *in utero*, the old brain is the first part of the brain to develop. Recent MRI studies on human development from birth to adulthood reveal that the new brain is not even finished until age twenty-four!

The old brain is well named, as it dates back to about 450 million years ago. According to leading neuroscientist Robert Ornstein in *The Evolution of Consciousness*, our old brain is concerned solely with our survival, as it has been for millions of years.

The body of research that demonstrates the prevalence of the old brain in the decision-making process is overwhelming. In the book *How the Brain Works*, human brain scientist Leslie Hart states, "Much evidence now indicates that the old brain is the main switch in determining what sensory input will go to the new brain, and what decisions will be accepted."

Antonio Damasio, a behavioral neurologist professor of neuroscience at the University of Southern California, and head of USC's Brain and Creativity Institute, states in his book, *Descartes' Error*, "Emotion, feeling, and biological regulation all play a role in human reason. The lowly orders of our organism are in the loop of higher reason." In other words, survival-related functions play a role in the decision-making process.

Michael Tomasello, a cognitive scientist and co-director of the Max Planck Institute for Evolutionary Anthropology in Germany, writes, "The 6 million years that separate human beings from other great apes is a very short time evolutionarily, with modern humans and chimpanzees sharing 99 percent of their genetic material. . . . There simply has not been enough time for normal processes of biological evolution involving genetic variation and natural selection to have created one by one each of the cognitive skills necessary for modern humans to invent and maintain complex tool-use industries and technologies, complex forms of symbolic communication."

Other works that highlight the role and importance of the old brain include *You've Got to Be Believed to Be Heard,* by Bert Decker, who develops the concept of achieving trust via the old brain in order to generate understanding, and *Emotional Intelligence*, by Daniel Goleman, who also reviews the working principals of the old brain. In *Emotional Brain*, Dr. Joseph LeDoux points out that the amygdala—located in the old brain—"has a greater influence on the cortex than the cortex has on the amygdala, allowing emotional arousal to dominate and control thinking."

With all this scientific evidence, the challenge in sales and marketing becomes: how do you address a brain that is 450 million years old? Sales people, politicians, educators, and even parents can testify how hard it is to convince people by simply using words. Words have been around for "only" about 40,000 years. Before that, man's communication was limited to a few grunts or gestures. It is even more difficult to try to influence your audience using written language. Why? Written words have only been around for about 10,000 years. That means the old brain is 45,000 times older than written words! There has not been enough time, in evolutionary terms, for written words to make an impact on our old brain.

So is it even possible to convince such a primitive organ using text?

To motivate and inspire our old brain, we must first learn to speak an entirely new language. This book is the only book to combine the latest brain research with cutting edge sales, marketing, and communication techniques.

WHAT TO REMEMBER

Researchers have demonstrated that human beings make decisions in an emotional manner and then justify them rationally. Furthermore, we now know that the final decision is actually triggered by the old brain, a brain that doesn't even understand words.

THE ONLY SIX STIMULI
THAT SPEAK TO
THE OLD BRAIN

*Think like a wise man but communicate
in the language of the people.*
~William Butler Yeats, Irish Poet

So how do you systematically reach the true decision-maker, the old brain? The old brain, in addition to processing input directly from the new brain and the middle brain, responds only to six very specific stimuli, which, if mastered, give you the key to unlocking the decision-making process.

1. Self-Centered

The old brain is responsive to anything pertaining to self. Why? It is completely self-centered. Think of the old brain as the center of "ME," with no patience or empathy for anything that does not immediately concern its own well-being and survival. If you were to have the misfortune of seeing someone injured right in front of your eyes, your old brain wouldn't really care: it couldn't afford to. It would be too busy being relieved that you were not the one who was hurt. Emotionally, of course, you might empathize or, rationally, you may be concerned about the consequences of what just occurred, but these reactions occur at the middle or new brain level.

This stimulus example explains why 100 percent of your message as a seller should focus on your audience, not on you. If you take a critical look at your typical presentation, your Web site, or even your brochures, you will find that a lot of content relates to your business, your people, your history, your values, and your mission statement—none of which is of any particular interest to the survival brain of your audience. Your audience must hear what you can do for them before they will pay any kind of attention to you.

2. Contrast

The old brain is sensitive to clear contrast, such as before/after, risky/safe, with/without, or fast/slow. Contrast allows the old brain to make quick, risk-free decisions. Without it, the old brain enters into a state of confusion leading to a delayed decision or no decision at all.

Fundamentally, the old brain is wired to pay attention to disruptions or changes of state. It is hard not to notice when someone enters a room, when a cellular phone vibrates or when a light is turned on. These sorts of disruptions may signal important cues to what is going on in our environment, so they receive some priority in the way they are processed by our old brain. In fact, as much as we believe we are *reactive* to changes or disruptions, scientists have actually proven that our senses *proactively* scan our surroundings for such pattern interrupters.

> Increase your selling probability by triggering the only six stimuli that reach the true decision-maker.

All of this means that you must create contrast to get your customers' old brain's attention. Using "neutral statements" such as "we are one of the leading providers of" is disastrous to your presentation. This type of language does not help your audience to quickly sort out information and trigger a decision.

3. Tangible Input

Since the old brain is not qualified to process written language, the use of words—especially complicated ones—will slow down the decoding of your message and automatically place the burden of information processing onto the new brain. Your audience will want to "think" about making the decision more than they will want to "act" on that decision.

This is why the old brain needs tangible input: It is constantly scanning for what is familiar and friendly, concrete and immutable, and recognizable. The old brain cannot process concepts like "a flexible

13

solution," "an integrated approach," or "scalable architecture" without a great deal of effort and skepticism. It appreciates simple, easy-to-grasp, concrete ideas like "more money," "unbreakable," and "24-hour turnaround time."

4. The Beginning and the End

Why do most of us remember the beginning and end of the movies we see and forget everything in the middle? The brain is constantly looking to conserve vital energy and will tend to drop information in the process. If the old brain can easily anchor a situation with a strong beginning point and a strong end point, it will not seek to use energy to retain content in the middle because it may not be necessary or vital to what the situation requires.

The old brain enjoys openings and finales and often overlooks what is in between. Such a short attention span has huge implications on how you as a seller should construct and deliver your messages. Placing the most important content at the beginning is a must, as is repeating it at the end. Anything in the middle of your message will be mostly overlooked.

Neuroscientists have recently discovered that there may be something else affecting our level of attention for specific events: it is simply the degree to which those events trigger one of the greatest forms of pleasure to our brains—anticipation. Indeed, when we anticipate, we actually produce more dopamine in an area called "the reward center," located in the old brain. The change of dopamine, a neurotransmitter, will raise our attention because it produces a natural high to our brain and improves our ability to retain and recall specific details of our experience. Recognizing the importance of this stimulus will give you a tremendous advantage over your competition. Should you have the choice of presenting first or last, you should always choose to present first, because you have an opportunity to anchor the first "beginning" point against which all other presentations will be measured. It is typically easier for people to assess content to be worse than better, so you stand a great chance of staying on top of the list!

5. VISUAL STIMULI

The old brain is visual. This may be because the optic nerve, which is physically connected to the old brain, is forty times faster than the auditory nerve, the nerve from the ear to the brain. Neuroscience demonstrates that when you see something that looks like a snake, your old brain warns you instantly of danger—in about two milliseconds—causing you to react even before your new brain physically recognizes the object is a snake. In fact, it will take about 500 milliseconds for the visual cortex part of your neocortex to recognize that indeed it is a snake. Neurons connect with one another at the speed of one millisecond, so the visual processing capability of our brain is near the speed of neuronal transmission. This makes the brain both extraordinarily fast and dangerously hasty. When we see a stick that looks like a snake, our old brain cannot afford to wonder if it is really a snake; it will highjack our entire body and trigger a movement to move us away from danger. This "low path processing" happens so fast that the higher functions of the brain are simply not informed. When the information crawls back up in our neocortex, the higher brain will perform a more sophisticated analysis of the situation. Still, a full 500 milliseconds will have passed until it concludes that the stick was not a snake.

Since humans cannot rely on the speed at which the new brain processes information, we are hardwired to make decisions that are mostly based on visual input. By using visual stimuli, you ensure that you tap into the processing bias that the brain has developed over thousands of years.

6. EMOTION

The old brain is only triggered by emotion. Thankfully, the field of neurobiology has brought more clarity to how our emotions work. Scientific studies show that emotions create electrochemical responses in our brains. These reactions directly impact the way we process and memorize information.

For example, we have over 100 billion neurons in the gray matter of our brain. The cells are not that extraordinary on their own. But when we experience an emotion like sadness, anger, joy, or surprise, a cocktail of hormones floods our brain and impacts the synaptic connections between our neurons, making them faster and stronger than ever before. As a result, we remember events better when we have experienced them with strong emotions.

If your customers cannot easily remember your message, how can you expect them to choose your product? That is why ignoring your audience's emotions is not an option. As Antonio Damasio says in *Descartes' Error*, "We are not thinking machines that feel, we are feeling machines that think."

The Only Six Stimuli that Speak to the Old Brain

Now you are familiar with the six stimuli that speak to the old brain. These six stimuli are universal and thus are powerful. Every person in the field of marketing and sales does well to develop his or her recipe for success with these key ingredients in mind.

> ## What to Remember
>
> The old brain responds to only six stimuli. Incorporating these six stimuli will give you fast access to the old brain and will immediately improve your ability to sell, market, and communicate.

THE METHODOLOGY: FOUR STEPS TO SUCCESS

Creating a new theory is not like destroying an old barn and erecting a skyscraper in its place. It is rather like climbing a mountain, gaining new and wider views, and discovering unexpected connections between our starting point and its rich environment.

~ALBERT EINSTEIN, PHYSICIST

To help you sell, market, and influence more effectively, we have translated the old brain's six stimuli into four easy, action-based steps. So your old brain can better remember these steps, we made them rhyme.

Four Fundamental Steps to Tap into the Old Brain

1. Diagnose the *Pain*.

2. Differentiate your *Claims*.

3. Demonstrate the *Gain*.

4. Deliver to the *Old Brain*.

Remember: *Pain, Claims, Gain, Old Brain!*

To better understand the four steps to increase selling, let's break them down just as we did with the old brain's six stimuli.

1. Diagnose the Pain

In this step you should ask the right questions and listen carefully to your prospects' answers. The true pain often lies below the conscious level, so be prepared to unveil pain your customers did not even know they had.

Since the old brain is self-centered and concerned with its own survival above all else, it is highly interested in solutions that will alleviate any pain it is feeling. That is why humans spend more time and energy avoiding pain or looking to destroy pain than we devote to gaining higher levels of comfort. Focus on the pain your prospect is experiencing, not the features of your products or service.

For example, if you're selling electric drills, your prospects couldn't care less about the actual drills. What they really want are holes. Therefore, your diagnostic or solution should focus on all the issues they have about the holes they need to make . . . not the drills. Combining your expert knowledge with their own understanding of their current situation and their desired outcome will lead to an accurate diagnostic of your customers' pain.

2. DIFFERENTIATE YOUR CLAIMS

Have you noticed that approximately 95 percent of all Web sites or brochures start with the same sentence: "We are one of the leading providers of . . ."? Such an empty claim or *neutral* statement works against you. To reach the old brain more effectively, you should say (and prove) a *contrasted* statement like, "We are the only provider of . . ."

As you have learned, the old brain responds favorably to clear, solid contrast. Powerful, unique claims attract prospects because they highlight the difference, gap, or disruption the old brain is pro-actively looking for to justify a quick decision. Claims simplify and accelerate purchasing decisions.

During every one of your sales pitches, your prospects will be thinking of two contrasting scenarios, regardless of whether they come up in your discussion:

- *How does this compare to other options?*
- *How does this compare to my doing nothing?*

So ask yourself, "Is my solution uniquely able to cure my prospects' pain?" If you can quickly point to what is absolutely different and valuable about your solution, you create the contrast that the old brain seeks. More importantly, you become the only vendor that can solve their pain.

3. DEMONSTRATE THE GAIN

Focusing on the unique benefits of your solution as recommended in Step Two is all well and good, but technically, it doesn't prove anything. Remember, the old brain prefers tangible information over complicated or abstract concepts. It needs solid proof of how your solution will enable it to survive or benefit. Since the old brain can't decide unless it feels secure, you need to concretely demonstrate, not just describe, the gain your prospects will experience from your product or service—the benefits of a specific cure to their pain—in a way that satisfies the old brain's need for concrete evidence.

Remember, when it comes to communicating the benefits of your solution (commonly called your value proposition), it's not just about value: it's about proven value!

4. DELIVER TO THE OLD BRAIN

The latest brain research shows that the old brain always makes the final call. This is why, when you deliver your message, your impact is directly linked to your ability to sell to the decision-making part of your prospects' brain. The language of the six stimuli will trigger a response because it is a language the old brain understands. In fact, your ability to deliver directly to the old brain affects your selling probability as much as the three other factors—pain, claims, and gain—combined.

Your Selling Probability =
Pain x Claim x Gain x (Old Brain)^3

The upcoming chapters will cover each of these action steps in greater detail. But first, let's go through the four steps in a simple sales example. Imagine for a moment that you are selling a commodity like water. How can you utilize the steps to stimulate your prospects' old brain to favor your product?

1. The more thirst—translate *pain*—your prospects are experiencing, the more potential you have to sell them the water.
2. If you have two competitors who also sell water, assuming that your claims are equally as strong as those of your two competitors, your selling probability is immediately divided by three.
3. Let's assume that your unique claim is that your water is the most refreshing. The more strongly you are able to prove what your customer will gain by drinking your "most refreshing" water, the greater your chance is to close the sale.
4. To stimulate your creativity, imagine you and your two competitors are selling water in the middle of a desert. As a way to impact your prospects' old brain, you could advertise your water using a large billboard with a fountain of actual cold water flowing out of it while giving away small samples for them to taste. This surely would have more impact than just using a small sign that said: "Fresh Water."

Applying the Four Steps of Selling to the Old Brain requires method and discipline, but the rewards are well worth the effort. Remember, these techniques are based on an innovative combination of the latest brain research and cutting-edge sales, marketing, and communication techniques. You should begin to use the techniques immediately, as they will help turn your newfound theoretical knowledge into messages that will compel your audience to buy from you.

WHAT TO REMEMBER

You will directly increase your chances to sell if you follow the four fundamental steps:

1. Diagnose the pain to craft a message that concretely shows how you can eliminate it.
2. Differentiate your claims by showing the contrast between you and your competitors
3. Demonstrate the gain that your solution provides to your prospect.
4. Deliver to the old brain in a way that has maximum impact.

STEP 1: DIAGNOSE THE PAIN

One of the best ways to persuade others is
with your ears—by listening to them.

~DEAN RUSK, FORMER US SECRETARY OF STATE

How would you feel if you were sick and your doctor prescribed a medicine without listening to you describe your symptoms first? How much faith would you have in his or her treatment plan? Similarly, how do you feel when a salesperson tries to sell you a product without understanding your pain or sources of stress and tension first?

Before prescribing medication, a doctor asks questions and typically initiates a dialogue that helps unveil the true source of a patient's pain. From this information, the doctor formulates a diagnosis and then explains it. Often the doctor makes sure the patient really understands and accepts the diagnosis. By doing so, the doctor can be more confident that he or she will follow instructions and take the prescribed medication.

By taking the time to carefully probe your prospects' pain, you achieve several goals:

- You help them unveil the true source of their pain.
- You establish your expertise by the appropriateness and relevance of your questions.
- You establish valuable trust with their old brain.

Years ago, a pizza company did a survey to uncover the number one pain of customers who ordered home-delivered pizza. What do you think it was? The taste of the pizza? How hot or cold it was? Getting it fast? Actually, the number one pain customers expressed was the anxiety of not knowing when the pizza would arrive. Armed with this vital information, Domino's Pizza established a very successful slogan: *Thirty minutes or less (or it's free)*. Such a savvy solution only came because they had diagnosed the pain of their prospects. Domino's recognized their customers' main problem (pain), and then showed them how they would solve it.

Can you and each of your coworkers state the number one pain of your prospects? Are you absolutely certain you are selling benefits that are correctly aligned with that primary pain?

Let's look at what happened to Christophe Morin, coauthor of this book, while heading the US subsidiary of a company that manufactures flags and signs. His main problem: how can you win a multi-million dollar, highly competitive American Olympic contract when you are a foreign-owned business with little US presence and your solution is the most expensive?

The answer is by doing the best diagnostic of your prospect's pain. Following is Christophe's account:

I spent two and a half years visiting ACOG (Atlanta Committee for the Olympic Games) from 1993 to 1996. It took this much time to understand ACOG's complex and ever-changing organizational chart and to discover the dominant financial, strategic, and personal expectations of the buying committee responsible for flags, flagpoles, flag ceremonies, and flag logistics.

This meticulous and tedious process led me to a surprising conclusion: ACOG's pain was mostly personal. Buyers were deeply worried about the embarrassing, if not devastating, impact of a diplomatic incident. Think about it: raising or flying a country's flag can be a delicate matter. For instance, what is the proper protocol for raising a flag in an indoor venue? How should it be handled and folded? Who will view the flag, and how will it appear from each angle? How high does it need to go logistically to be seen properly? How do you make sure that the design of a particular country has been officially approved or updated?

These are the exact pain factors I focused on. During the development of the RFQ (Request for Quote), I insisted that we had the highest level of competency in the art and science of flags (vexillology) and could claim to be the only company in the world that had developed an officially approved digital database of flag designs. By clearly and comprehensively articulating these unique claims—and address-ing an obvious and profound understanding of ACOG's pain—I was able to overcome the overwhelming odds against us and close a multi-million-dollar deal.

With Christophe's story in mind, let's investigate the best way to diagnose the pain. To properly diagnose a prospect's pain, you simply need to answer the following four questions:

1. What is the source of the prospect's most prominent pain?
2. What is the intensity of that pain?
3. What is the level of urgency requiring the pain to be solved?
4. Is my prospect aware of and does he/she acknowledge his/her own pain?

Each of these questions must be answered correctly to make a cor-rect diagnosis.

1. WHAT IS THE SOURCE OF THE PAIN?

Knowing the source of the pain helps qualify the amount of tension or stress that is driving the intent to buy. Pain always falls into three main categories: financial, strategic, and personal.

Financial pain covers your prospect's economic performance or lack thereof. It is typically highly visible and easy to measure. Sales rev-enues, profitability, and ROI (Return On Investment) are good indi-cators of a prospect's financial health.

Strategic pain includes issues that affect the business processes used to develop, manufacture, and sell products or services. Typical strategic types of pain include poor product quality, declining market share, and higher business risk. This type of pain is not as visible or easily measured as financial pain.

Personal pain is made up of the feelings and emotions affecting those who are involved in deciding how and when to resolve the prospect's primary pain. High stress levels, job insecurity, and longer working days are all good examples of possible personal pain.

Defining the source of the pain is like taking a patient's pulse at the right location. It is the best way to make sure your product or service is designed to bring effective relief. As you seek to find the pain source and

> Assess whether the pain is Financial, Strategic, or Personal.

continue on through the other diagnostic questions, keep in mind that the first level of diagnosing the pain is best performed through extensive marketing research.

Research can be conducted both to *explore* pain and to *measure* it. In both instances, using surveys that ask the right questions is critical. The person or organization designing the survey must not focus too much on descriptive variables like demographics. Instead, they should seek to find motivational variables—fears, desires, expectations, attitudes, and satisfactions. These answers will unveil the real pain.

It will probably take anywhere from twelve to sixteen interviews to *explore* your prospect's pain. Since your sample is so small, make sure you select very different individuals to interview. Stretching the boundaries of factors responsible for the pain is absolutely essential to producing a good qualitative assessment.

To *measure* pain, depending on the total size of your market, you will need bigger samples. Most Business to Consumer markets will require at least three hundred respondents to draw statistically meaningful results. At that sample size, there is a 95 percent confidence level that the actual population mean is within about 10 percent of the sample mean. For instance, on a yes-or-no question, if your mean is 20 percent for yes, you can be 95 percent confident that the actual mean would be between a minimum of 10 percent and a maximum of 30 percent if you were to survey the entire population.

> Learn to detect and focus on the high-intensity pain.

In addition to making sure you have enough respondents, pay attention to your interviewing methods. Conduct interviews over the telephone, on the Web, face-to-face, or in a combination of all three for best results. Note, however, that for the above statistics to apply, your sample must be random, or nearly so. Therefore, it is not wise to include only volunteer respondents.

2. WHAT IS THE INTENSITY OF THE PAIN?

The intensity of the pain is a crucial factor—you don't want to waste your time offering a cure for what may be a temporary itch. As you diagnose your prospect's pain, learn to measure its intensity. Low intensity is typically related to a low involvement or low urgency in the buying decision process. If the prospect or organization will not commit major resources such as time, people, or money to the resolution of the pain, they may be hard to convince that they need a "cure" or a solution.

High-intensity pain manifests itself when large amounts of resources or efforts are drawn by the pain. Pinpoint whether the pain you are working to eliminate is of high or low intensity early in your selling process. Then focus on the high-intensity pain!

3. How urgent is the need to alleviate the pain?

After you have identified the source and intensity of your prospect's pain, you will know whether or not your prospect has powerful and compelling reasons to seek an imminent cure for the pain. Urgency is a direct function of the consequences that will be felt if the pain is not cured.

> Focus on the most time-sensitive pain areas.

If the consequences are imminent or growing proportionately, then your prospect is more likely to act sooner than later. If there is not enough urgency, then your prospect's old brain will postpone a decision in order to deal with other priorities related to survival.

4. Does my prospect acknowledge the pain?

It is critical to the selling process for your prospect to acknowledge his or her own pain. Many times a customer's common or obvious pain will have multiple solutions from several competitors. So be sure to uncover a pain that is more unique or previously unrecognized and give the prospect time to acknowledge it. This will open a new door in their consciousness of the buying options. As a result, once they agree with your assessment of their pain, they will easily buy into your solution.

> Ensure that your prospect acknowledges his or her pain.

Think about the last time you went to see a doctor. Probably after answering questions related to your ailment, you were asked to confirm that the doctor's diagnosis was realistic and reasonable. If you agreed with the diagnosis, you were much more likely to accept the recommended treatment plan as well.

In the sales and marketing arena, once you have assessed a prospect's primary pain along with its source, measured the intensity of that pain and the interest in alleviating it, and gotten your prospect to agree with your assessment, you are in position to offer an effective, on-target solution. The following case scenario shows such a process (see Figure 4-1).

Many sales and marketing teams make the mistake of only pro-

PAIN FACTOR

SOURCE	INTENSITY	TIMING	AWARENESS
Mainly Financial	High	Immediate	High
Loss of Money	Prospect is allocating multiple resources to eliminate the PAIN	Prospect's life or business will endure instant deterioration if no action is taken	Prospect is highly conscious and actively seeking a solution

FIGURE 4-1

moting specific features of their product or service. More experienced marketers may transform those features into benefits. Experts, however, will creatively diagnose their prospect's pain and then address this pain with a solution that is customized and unique.

Sony once created an ad for video projectors that focused on one very specific pain they had identified: the projectors were heavy to carry. An ad like theirs (see Figure 4-2), which featured the world of

FIGURE 4-2

the prospects, enhanced the pain or trauma that the prospects already felt. Notice how emphasizing a prospect's pain can have much higher impact on the old brain than simply featuring the benefits of the projector or even picturing the projector itself. This works because the prospect's old brain can relate to the self-centered, visual pain that is reenacted in the ad.

> Start your sales process with open-ended questions.

Also note the power of focusing on one main benefit of a projector: its small size and light weight. An actual projector isn't even visible in the picture. By reenacting the target group's pain—not by emphasizing the features of Sony's projector—this ad speaks directly to the old brain.

More Diagnostic Tips

Your approach in discovering the answers to the four pain-related questions is critical. Following are some tips for getting the answers you seek.

Ask Open Questions

In the diagnostic phase of the sales process, you should always start by asking open-ended questions—questions that cannot be answered with "yes" or "no." These types of questions invite your prospects to reflect on their pain and eventually come to acknowledge its severity and/or urgency.

Keep in mind that, at this early stage, you should drive the diagnostic without real attachment to winning the business: if your prospect's pain cannot be cured by your product or service, then you should move on and look for another prospect. The soft-selling approach adds great credibility for you and builds trust for the future. On the other hand, if your product or service can solve the top pain of the prospect, then communicate the unique benefits of your products, i.e., your claims, early in the sales cycle to inevitably disqualify your competitors.

Seek to Understand, Get Feedback

Manuel Hoffmann is a director of marketing at a high-tech company in Silicon Valley. His favorite tool to help jumpstart the dialogue with his prospects is to invite them to use a whiteboard.

"In my first meetings with them," Hoffman says, "I really want to understand their pain. As I listen to their issues and challenges, I often draw a picture on the whiteboard. Then I ask them if this is correct, and I hand them the pen. It's amazing what people are willing to reveal if you are willing to listen and truly understand their pain points."

Perfect Your Diagnostic Dialogue

If your process allows for an individual interview with your prospect, you should adopt a "Diagnostic Dialogue" technique. In his renowned book *On Dialogue*, world-famous quantum physicist Dr. David Bohm offers four fundamental rules to conducting an effective dialogue. In order to explore your prospect's pain and make an accurate assessment of that pain, you should use these four principles, which ensure the optimum flow of ideas and thoughts toward quick understanding:

PRINCIPLES OF EFFECTIVE DIALOGUE

1. SUSPEND JUDGMENT

By holding back your opinions, you release the tight grip on your pre-conceived positions. You create a climate of trust and intimacy in which your prospect feels free to open up and take a good look at his or her situation.

2. LISTEN DEEPLY

True listening means that you allow others' ideas and opinions to influence yours. Convey this willingness to your prospects through your attention and your body movement. Remember to actively search for the meaning behind your prospects' words rather than impatiently waiting for them to stop speaking so you can jump in with your own thoughts. The way you listen will directly impact your capacity to learn and build quality pain diagnostics.

3. CHALLENGE ASSUMPTIONS

Assumptions are like dirty glasses. When we look through them, we sometimes draw wrong conclusions about what we see. Our perception may be distorted by our own experience. It is always wise to state your assessment—with the awareness that it is your perception—and make sure the other person in the dialogue sees it the same way. Openly discussing your assumptions enables you to build your dialogue from a platform of truth and clarity.

> Use Diagnostic Dialogue as a shortcut to assess the main pain of your prospect.

4. INQUIRE AND REFLECT

Inquiry brings new information. Reflection brings new meaning to the information and creates a new understanding of the relationships between various pieces of information. If you reflect on what your prospect says by accurately restating his or her points, you not only can assure him that you understand his pain, you can also probe into her problem deeper, to learn further details. This fosters an environment for creative thinking that builds on past experiences instead of reliving the same pattern over and over again. In short, it creates new ideas.

PUTTING IT ALL TOGETHER

Sales and marketing professionals who are strong in selling to the old brain apply these diagnostic rules naturally. Because they create a safe climate, the prospects often follow suit, leading to a deeper dialogue and a greater opportunity to discover the prospects' real pain.

Take heed: a common mistake made during sales discussions is to start selling too early. Selling too early without a diagnostic is like trying to provide a cure when you don't know the exact disease. If you jump into a description of features and benefits without taking the time to assess

> Selling without a thorough diagnostic is like providing a cure when you're not sure what the disease is.

the pain, you may be wasting your breath. Your prospect may assume that you are specialized only in one particular area or that your offer is peripheral to what they really need: a cure for their most acute pain.

That is why, during your initial visits to your prospects, your main challenge is not to give a sales pitch but rather to conduct a thorough pain diagnostic. Remember the four Rules of Dialogue: (1) suspend judgment, (2) listen deeply, (3) challenge assumptions, and (4) inquire and reflect.

For more measurable and tangible results, you should conduct a formal marketing survey that will help you unveil the true pain by asking deeper motivational questions. Once again, it is critical that your prospects' pain is brought to their awareness.

Even if you sell the same products to different groups or types of people, this is not a one-size-fits-all diagnostic process: your prospects' pain may differ significantly from one group to another. To address clusters of prospects, confirm and verify the common pain of each cluster. If you are selling to individual prospects, confirm the pain for each individual prospect. If you are selling to a group, you may need to confirm the personal pain of each one of the decision-influencers.

In *How Customers Think*, Gerald Zaltman, professor at Harvard Business School, states, "Marketers need methods that go beyond what a customer can readily articulate—that get at what people don't know they know . . . the more important is the unconscious mind."

It all begins with a careful diagnostic of the pain.

What to Remember

Avoid the mistake of attempting to sell too soon. Not having a thorough diagnostic is like trying to prescribe medication for someone when you don't even know their symptoms. If you begin to describe the features and functions of your solution without taking the time to evaluate the pain of your prospect, he or she may end up believing your solution is too specific or too narrow, and therefore not effective in curing the pain. Above all else, your solution must address your prospect's deepest pain.

STEP 2: DIFFERENTIATE YOUR CLAIMS

In order to be irreplaceable one must always be different.
~COCO CHANEL, FASHION DESIGNER

If you are not selling something unique, you are selling as much for your competitors as you are for yourself. So, what is distinctive about your product or service?

It is vital to define what is unique about your product or service before you can get the attention of the old brain. As you'll recall, contrast is one of the six stimuli that impacts the old brain. Claims

41

create the evidence of a sharp contrast between your solution and all others offered by your competition.

When your prospect hears, "We are one of the leading providers of . . ." this claim fails entirely to impact the old brain. Why? It offers no contrast. The highest impact on the old brain is achieved when you say, "We are the only provider of . . . "

Sometimes it is a challenge to find a unique angle when selling. Take bread, for example. Could there be a more general product? Is there a more saturated market than the bread business in Paris? Isn't bread in Paris the ultimate commodity product? Let's consider the habits of two bread buyers I happen to know.

For years, my father has driven two miles every day to go to the same bakery, in a country where bread shops are on every corner. Why? He believes that bakery has the best bread in the area. The quality of their bread is known to be unique, and my dad is so fanatic about bread that he is willing to drive the extra distance.

In contrast, when I lived in Paris, 99 percent of the time I bought my bread from the bakery downstairs from my apartment. Although the bread at the downstairs bakery was only average, my main buying criteria was the fact that I didn't have to make any detour to buy my daily baguette—it was literally on the same sidewalk as my parking exit. I often came back late from work, and after a long, stressful day, the idea of saving a few minutes of time was enough to keep me as a faithful customer. This bakery was the only bakery between the parking garage exit

> Always sell something that is perceived to be totally unique.

and the elevator that led to my apartment—a unique benefit for me when my pain was arriving home late.

So every time you walk into a coffee shop or lunch spot, ask yourself, "What is special about this place that makes me buy here?" You'll quickly notice there is always something unique that explains your buying decision.

If you recognize the role uniqueness plays for you as a buyer, what about the role it plays in your work with sales and marketing? How do you as a seller pinpoint and convey your unique claims? The answer is simple: pretend you are an inventor.

When inventors wish to register an invention, they must go through an extensive patent registration process that culminates in the description of what are called "claims."

In this process, an inventor must argue that certain features or benefits of his invention have not been offered by any previous inventions. After all, an invention is not an invention unless it is unique. The patent process demands that any features claimed as new must be contrasted with what already exists.

In the marketing sector, treat your solution as an invention and build your message firmly on your claims. Remember to focus on what

> Claim that you are the only one who does or has something specific.

is unique about your offering, how it contrasts with other competitors. Let's turn once again to video projector ads for some real world examples of how leading companies choose their claims and highlight them:

Main Claim: Our Projector Is the Smallest

Remember the earlier ad that focused on the prospect's pain of carrying heavy, large projectors? Here is an example of another ad (see Figure 5-1) that focuses on the same claim—having the smallest and lightest projector—but uses a different approach.

In the EVOLUTION of Technology

It's about Survival of the SMALLEST

© 2003 Frédéric Neema

With our projector, size DOES matter

The 3999 series ProjectX projector is the smallest on the market. When you need to present, it fits right in a briefcase with room to spare. Don't get bogged down by dragging a dinosaur everywhere you go.

PROJECTX

FIGURE 5-1

Main Claim: Our Projector Is the Brightest

In this ad, the claim is all about the brightness of the image the projector displays (see Figure 5-2). The pain being addressed is how poorly an image from another brand of projector shows up in brightly lit rooms. To differentiate yourself from the competition, choose one

FIGURE 5-2

main claim that correlates with your prospect's pain and address it in a powerful way. You can't miss the evident claim in this ad of being the "brightest" projector on the market.

Main Claim: Our Projector Is the Easiest to Use

A third pain uncovered in the world of projectors is the difficulty of setting them up and using them.

In the examples we just reviewed, notice how each manufacturer differentiates its claims. They aren't selling "just another video projector." Instead, they are selling

- The smallest projector,
- The brightest projector, or
- The easiest projector to use.

By focusing on a specific claim, each company emphasizes its own strength to disqualify the competition.

WHAT IS UNIQUE ABOUT YOUR SOLUTION?

If you have difficulties finding something unique about your business, look beyond pure technology or service differences. Be creative when you make your claims. For a creative sampling, see if you recognize some of the different marketing angles used by the following companies:

- The Original, like Coca Cola or Levi's.
- The Recommended Choice, as in "recommended by more doctors."

- Genuine, like Russian vodka or German cars.
- Convenience, like pre-washed lettuce or one-stop shopping.
- Number One in Sales (at the time), Hertz rental car.

AVIS'S UNIQUE CLAIM

How would you establish a unique claim for your rental car company if you were not number one in sales? Traditionally, every rental car company rents out the same cars from the same airport counters, and their services and pricing are almost identical.

Avis creatively found something unique about being number two to then-leader Hertz. The slogan Avis adopted, "We Try Harder," implies that you will receive better service from them than from any of their competitors.

> Treat your solution as an invention, and build your message firmly on your claims.

"We Try Harder" landed Avis the distinction of having the most recognized brand slogan in the rental car industry. Launched in 1963, "We Try Harder" has become synonymous with Avis, superior customer service, and going the extra mile.

The ubiquitous "We Try Harder" button is worn not only by Avis employees, but is often adopted by volunteers of different charities to highlight the volunteers' spirit. It was even embraced in a camouflage version by US soldiers fighting in Vietnam.

Once you find a unique message about your product or service, the possibilities are endless.

WHAT TO REMEMBER

Find one or several unique attributes about your solution so you can strongly assert your claims. Claims that eliminate the strongest principal pain of your prospects will best motivate them to buy from you.

STEP 3: DEMONSTRATE THE GAIN

Tell a man there are 300 billion stars in the universe, and he'll believe you. Tell him the plate you're handing him is very hot, and he'll have to touch it to believe you.

~MIKE JAEGER, MUSICIAN

By this stage of our neuromarketing journey, you have properly diagnosed the pain of your prospects and discovered what unique claims you can make to position your offering as the best cure. Your next task, then, is to demonstrate that your prospects will get a substantial gain when they choose your product or your service.

There are over 1,200 books that talk about the Value Proposition—it's likely that you've read some of them. The main point they communicate is that to do a good job in presenting your Value Proposition, all you need to do is to highlight the highest possible value your solution may bring to your prospect. Unfortunately, they all omit the importance of reaching the old brain. Simply "highlighting" the value is not enough; you have to *prove it.*

> Don't just talk about your gain; prove it!

Because it controls our most primitive survival mechanisms, the true decision-maker, the old brain, is especially resistant to adopting new ideas or behaviors. Some research has even suggested that the pain of making a change may be as harsh as physical torture to some minds.

How does one combat such resistance? Be tangible and provide hard evidence.

You may think that because your product or service provides great value, it should sell itself. If the benefits of your solution are greater than its cost (the gain), your prospects would be foolish not to buy it from you. However, no matter how much sense (and cents) this solution may make to you, the old brain requires proof.

A few years ago I was hired to help a start-up company raise money. Their product was a new device for portable phones or palm-tops, which they believed had the potential to become the *de facto* standard for all wireless devices of the future.

We scheduled our first meeting with two people from a venture capital firm. John and Ron were using a large suite in a hotel by the airport where they had filled their entire agenda for the day with presentations from seven different start-ups. At 4:00 p.m., our allotted time slot, we knocked on their door.

Step 3: Demonstrate the Gain

They greeted us professionally, but with a definite lack of enthusiasm. We were the last to present that day, and when Ron joked about the fact that we were the "last obstacle before their shower, a hot meal, and what would be a well-deserved night of sleep," I knew we had our work cut out for us.

As we set up for our presentation, John shared a little about how their day had gone. He said, "All six products we've seen today have great value propositions. All six founders are experienced and very enthusiastic, and all six of them have a perfectly laid-out plan of how they will go public in six to twelve months."

Then John volunteered some more information—that they were not particularly excited about making an investment in any of the companies they had seen because, in his words, "They've told us that their product is great and that there is a huge market for it. They've shown us the numbers they project . . . but they haven't actually proven anything."

Considering this new information and the seriousness of the situation, my client and I decided to skip our introduction and start directly with a proof of our value—an actual demo of our product.

We had a small prototype that perfectly illustrated what the product could do. It was so simple to use that the demo did not require any training and could be used instantly by anybody.

I handed the device to John. It took about five seconds before he excitedly said, "This is cool! I get it!"

John and Ron spent the next forty-five minutes playing with the different demos in the prototype. My client and I were beginning to think we were going to run out of time before we had a chance to tell them about the technology and the market.

We left their room at 6:45 p.m. that day with a commitment from them that they would send a team of their experts to review the technology and the nature of the investment. The prototype demo was an instant proof of value for John and Ron. Instead of just claiming value, we had actually proven the value of our claims.

A couple of months later, my client had raised all the money he needed.

THE VALUE MUST OUTWEIGH THE COSTS

When a prospect decides to make a purchase, there is always a cost involved—whether it is financial, strategic, or personal. Therefore, it is vital that you demonstrate the gain in a manner that can't be disputed. Gain can be defined as the value of your solution minus its cost. If your prospect's old brain does not perceive a relevant and tangible gain from your solution, it will never make the decision to buy.

Just like pain, gain can be broken down into three categories: financial, strategic, and personal.

1. *The Financial Gain* or *ROI* is proven when prospects see the evidence of measurable positive return on their purchase, such as saving money, increasing revenue, or boosting profits.

2. *The Strategic Gain* includes benefits that are less measurable yet provide strategic enhancements to their business, such as increased quality, faster product diversification, shorter market cycles, or easier access to new markets. This gain cannot always be translated into financial gain.

3. *The Personal Gain* relates to greater peace of mind, more fun, higher pride of ownership, improved chances for a promotion, a

greater sense of accomplishment, or more self-satisfaction. In a recent ad, IBM used this concept (see Figure 6-1) to illustrate the stress points an executive might personally experience in his life. Viewers

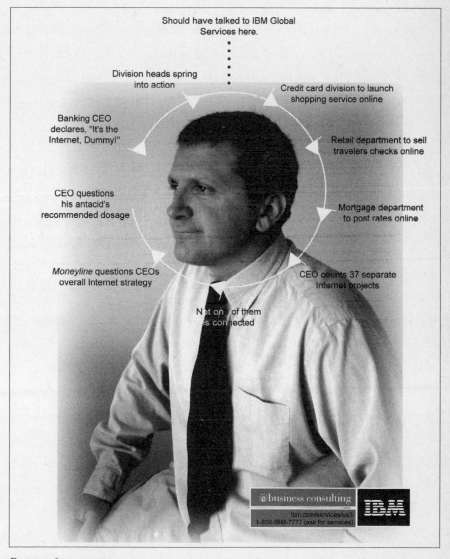

FIGURE 6-1

can immediately relate to the multitude of thoughts and worries in progression around him.

Four Ways to Prove the Gain

There are four ways to effectively demonstrate your offering's gain to the old brain. They are listed below from most effective to least effective. The effectiveness of each proof is largely a function of how easy it is for your prospects to believe it.

1. *A Customer Story: 80-100% Proof*

Imagine you are trying to sell your amazing product to Ford, and you have the benefit of already having sold a similar system to Chrysler. If you do a good job of illustrating Chrysler's gain in a tangible way, how easy do you think it will be for Ford to draw a parallel between the benefits Chrysler is deriving from your system and the benefits Ford could gain as well?

Customer stories are the strongest possible proof of gain. But choose your story wisely. The customer you choose as your example should share many common traits with your potential buyer. For example, you could say, "ABC company has been using our system for over three months now and has saved an average of five cents per transaction." Since your prospect manufactures similar products and does ten thousand transactions per day, they can infer that they would potentially save five hundred dollars per day or $175,000 per year.

Of course, a story coming directly from the customer in the form of a testimonial is even more powerful than having your prospect take your word for it. Hearing of your success from a peer in the following format will have even more impact: "We have been able to save five cents per transaction since we installed this new system."—John Smith, VP Operations, ABC Company. (A bit more compelling than, "We are completely satisfied with their system.")

In his book *The Psychology of Persuasion*, Arizona State University psychology professor Robert Cialdini cites the law of social reinforcement as one of the six ways to influence people. The law of social reinforcement stipulates that if we become aware that other people have already accepted a solution to an idea, our natural response will be to more easily accept this solution or idea for ourselves. A customer story is the strongest proof because it is provided by a third party and it is not making any assumption. It has already happened.

2. A Demo: 60–100% Proof

A demo is a short demonstration or prototype of your product or service that proves the gain without necessarily going through all of its features and functionality. In essence, it shows one particular benefit or unique quality. For the previous example, you could show that your prospect could save ten seconds per transaction, potentially creating a five-cent savings per transaction. Sometimes even a simple picture or a written document from a credible source can constitute a strong proof of gain.

Your demos must be perfectly scripted and rehearsed to make sure they don't fail. Depending on the strength of your demo, using it as a proof of gain can be highly effective.

The following ad (Figure 6-2) presents a strong demonstration of the proof of value:

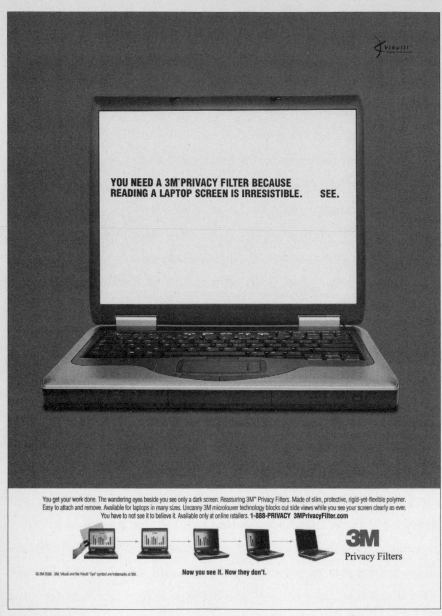

FIGURE 6-2

3. *Data: 20–60% Proof*

We have all slept through presentations where the speaker spouted out statistic after meaningless statistic. But when used properly, targeted data can work. Take the following financial calculation as a demonstration of gain:

> *Our product will save you an average of five cents per transaction. Since you average ten thousand transactions a day, you will save five hundred dollars a day—or $175,000 per year.*

This calculation is based on two assumptions:

1. Your prospect is making ten thousand transactions per day. If this number has been provided by your prospect, then he/she will find it credible and tangible.
2. Your solution can truly save them five cents per transaction. This assumption may be harder to justify without testimonials or a solid demo, but it helps put a dollar sign to the value.

You run a higher risk of your prospects' old brain raising questions and concerns when you give it data than you do when you share customer stories or run demos. Data means numbers, which do not have as much impact on the old brain. It's fine to use data if you don't have other options, but don't consider it a first-choice strategy. Data works best if you can use it to contrast a situation, like before and after.

Let's look at this attention-grabbing law firm ad (Figure 6-3); the proof of value that they bring is indeed data:

JUSTICE

MAY BE BLIND.

BUT SHE STILL

SEES IT OUR WAY

92.3%

OF THE TIME.

quinn emanuel trial lawyers LOS ANGELES · NEW YORK · SAN FRANCISCO · SILICON VALLEY · SAN DIEGO · PALM SPRINGS

FIGURE 6-3

4. A Vision: 10–40% Proof

Steve Jobs, founder of Apple Computers, was able to sell a vision of user-friendly, trendy computers well before the technology could be demonstrated. How?

By creating an irresistible vision.

Imagine you are targeting a large car manufacturer with a new device that makes the use of a gearbox or an automatic transmission totally obsolete. If you don't have a sale or a customer testimonial yet, you may choose a vision to demonstrate the gain. For example, you could say, "When the first CD players became available, people did not immediately recognize their value. Twenty years later, turntables are nearly extinct, and cassettes are fading fast. In the same way, our new transmission will render obsolete all previous technologies that transfer energy from the engine to the wheels."

Step 3: Demonstrate the Gain

When you have no other way to demonstrate the gain, a vision may help persuade your prospects that your solution will benefit them. Tell a story, use a metaphor, or create an analogy like the one above for the greatest effect. But remember that this type of proof requires that your prospect act on faith, and is therefore much less effective than other techniques.

Less effective, but still persuasive if done right. For example, take a look at an ad (Figure 6-4) from another law firm. Can you see that

Sanders, Lyn & Ragonetti Associates, Trial Lawyers

202-195 County Court Blvd. Brampton, Ontario L6W-4P7 Tel:(905)450-1711 Fax:(905)450-7066 www.slra.com

FIGURE 6-4

the proof of value they bring is a vision? Even though they don't really have a proof, they want you to believe that you'll win big if you work with them as a trial lawyer—and their ad probably triggered some emotion in your brain instantly!

ORGANIZE YOUR PROOFS OF GAIN

Organizing your proofs of gain in the form of a matrix (see Figure 6-5) helps your prospects determine if they can derive most of the gain from the financial, strategic, or personal area. It also helps you see if you are providing your prospects with tangible proofs, or if you are asking them to recognize your value by faith alone.

For each gain statement, you need at least one proof of gain. To

Proof of GAIN Matrix for Your CLAIMS				
Proof / Gain	Customer Story	Demo	Data	Vision
Financial				
Strategic				
Personal				

FIGURE 6-5

strengthen that proof—especially if you believe a particular gain is significant—you can use more than one piece of evidence.

For example, a prospect whose pain is primarily financial will be highly interested in how much money your solution will save. In this case, in addition to using a demo, you will make a much greater impact by including a powerful corresponding testimonial from a prior customer who experienced significant financial gain.

You have two effective options when presenting the proof of gain to prospects: You can follow the matrix vertically by telling a story that includes all three categories—financial, strategic, and personal—or you can use the matrix horizontally by giving multiple proofs in any one of the four categories.

Your matrix does not have to be complex. In fact, one element of the matrix can be a simple sentence like, "John Smith, VP of Manufacturing at ABC, saved his company $125,000 last year while using our new machine." You can devise longer and more complicated demonstrations of the gain. However, by keeping it simple, you will help your prospect's old brain accept the value statement.

Remember, the proofs of gain are the core of your message. As supporting evidence of your claims, they must be tangible, factual, and provable in order to impact your prospect's old brain. Make sure that every piece of information you share with your prospect has value for them. Ask yourself, "Am I training them on features and benefits, or am I actually selling something that will appeal to their old brain? Do I need to include this information to help them reach a decision, or am I just diluting my value with needless details?" These four words say it all: Don't just tell, *sell*!

Let's review a previous projector ad to dissect how they communicated their proof of gain.

Main claim: Our Projector Is Small.

Remember the ad on page 44 that featured a projector between books (Figure 5-1)? What kind of gain does an ad which focuses on the size of the projector allude to: financial, strategic, or personal?

The answer is personal gain: It suggests that by choosing a product from that particular manufacturer, you won't have to personally, physically drag a heavy, bulky projector with you whenever you're on the road.

The power of that ad lies primarily in how it focuses on the personal pain: all other features of the projector were deliberately omit-

Proof of GAIN Matrix for Your CLAIMS				
Proof / Gain	Customer Story	Demo	Data	Vision
Financial				
Strategic				
Personal		✓		

FIGURE 6-6

ted. The proof of gain was entirely based on one claim—the small size of the projector.

Now let's wrap this chapter up with some good news for all of you salespeople who abhor being pushy or manipulative: Sales books often present arguments or "tricks" to create urgency in your prospects' minds and push them to make faster buying decisions. But if you as a salesperson create a strong proof of gain, you will never have to worry about fostering that urgency—it will already be built right into your message. Why would your prospects delay the decision to buy if you have proven beyond reasonable doubt, visually and concretely, everything they will gain when they buy your solution?

WHAT TO REMEMBER

Simply talking about your product or service's value is not enough: you have to prove it. Conquer the old brain's doubts with tangible proof of gain through hard evidence: relevant customer testimonials, demonstrations, contrasting data, and/or a compelling vision. A simple matrix helps you and your customer see concretely the possibilities for financial, strategic, and personal gain. Remember: Don't just tell, *sell!*

STEP 4: DELIVER TO THE OLD BRAIN

*Power is not revealed by striking hard
or often, but by striking true.*

~HONORÉ DE BALZAC, FRENCH AUTHOR

If your prospects were rational, thinking robots, sales and marketing strategies would only include the first three steps of Selling to the Old Brain: Diagnosing the Pain, Differentiating Your Claims, and Demonstrating the Gain. However, human beings are not fully rational. All final decisions are made by our old brain.

That is why it is critical that you deliver your message in a manner that will directly impact the brain's true decision-maker. But how do you speak to the old brain? True, you must be unique by differentiating your claims and prove your value by demonstrating the gain. But these steps alone are not enough. The most solid and logical message, though it may interest your prospect, will not trigger a buying decision unless the old brain understands and remembers it. Even high-tech, high-dollar demos may be viewed by the old brain as a long list of features with no real connection to a tangible gain or a solution for the pain.

You must find a way to deliver your message with maximum impact.

And now, the good news: We have already found the way for you. Years of experience have taught us what tools you will need to construct those targeted, high-impact messages.

All you need is a toolbox.

BUILDING AND DELIVERING YOUR MESSAGE

Often when people get ready to deliver their message, they think about sentences or PowerPoints they should use. But focusing on words alone is limiting, as words have little or no impact on the old brain. The tools in your Selling to the Old Brain toolbox will help you go beyond words. For every message you create, you can utilize methods from two sets of tools in your Selling to the Old Brain toolbox to gain immediate attention and credibility.

The first set of tools is called the *Six Message Building Blocks*. Every worthwhile builder knows that a home is only as good as its foundation. Even the miraculous human body is composed of building blocks called cells. In the same way, the ultimate construction of a powerful message depends on the critical components of the Six Message Building Blocks.

These building blocks are foundational to creating a strategy that

Step 4: Deliver to the Old Brain

will reach the ever-important old brain. Like a reliable screwdriver or a tried-and-true hammer, they will come through for you time and again when preparing for a prospect presentation.

THE SIX "SELLING TO THE OLD BRAIN" MESSAGE BUILDING BLOCKS

1. Grabber
2. Big Picture
3. Claims
4. Proofs of Gain
5. Handling Objections
6. The Close

The second set of tools is called the *Impact Boosters*. They further boost the impact of each of your message building blocks so they will reach the old brain even faster. Enhancing the building blocks for maximum impact, they make your presentation more meaningful and memorable. If the six building blocks are your home's foundation that allow it to be secure and grounded, the seven impact boosters are the "window dressings" that make the house more appealing.

THE SEVEN IMPACT BOOSTERS

1. Wording with "You"
2. Your Credibility
3. Emotions
4. Contrast

5. Varying Learning Styles
6. Stories
7. Less Is More

The following chapters contain an in-depth discussion of each of these valuable tools. The more Selling to the Old Brain tools you use when you build and deliver your message, the more immediate impact you will have on your audience's old brain—ultimately helping you close deals and dramatically increasing your selling probability.

WHAT TO REMEMBER

The final and most crucial step in Selling to the Old Brain involves knowing how to deliver, or speak, to the old brain. We have researched six core components to help you do that; we call them building blocks. To enhance your message style and delivery, we will also share with you seven impact boosters. Get ready to learn!

THE FIRST MESSAGE
BUILDING BLOCK:
GRABBERS

If you grab attention in the first frame with a visual surprise,
you stand a better chance of holding the viewer.
~DAVID OGILVY, ADVERTISING EXPERT

For survival reasons, it is in the best interest of your old brain to be most alert at the beginning and end of interactions, in case change or an unknown new factor could cause danger. This is why the "bookends of a discussion" is one of the six stimuli to the old brain, which tends to pay less attention once security and familiarity are established. Once the old brain becomes comfortable, it often goes into a sort of energy-saving mode and pays less attention to its surroundings.

Knowing this, it is crucial to make a powerful impression early. If you do not grab your prospects' attention early in the interaction, you may lose them forever. This guideline applies equally to all forms of communication, including phone calls, faxes, e-mails, Web sites, cold calls, and face-to-face presentations.

As the conversation continues, strive to keep the old brain's attention. Recall the last time you attended a seminar or convention. At the beginning of each presentation, your old brain was wide-awake and on guard, scanning for the new and unfamiliar. In this mode, you achieved between 70 and 100 percent of maximum attention and retention.

As the presentation continued and your old brain perceived that nothing seemed to be threatening its survival, it dropped its guard and went into "idle mode." At that point, your attention and retention dropped to 20 percent of the maximum level (Figure 8-1), as demon-

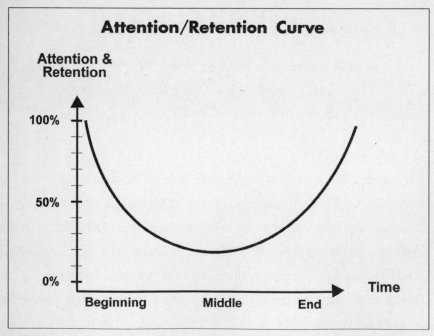

FIGURE 8-1

strated by George Morrisey and Thomas Sechrest in their book *Loud and Clear: How to Prepare and Deliver Effective Business and Technical Presentations*.

Now, think about the last time you gave a presentation. Did you start with one of the following topics?

1. Who you are or what your background is
2. The agenda of your presentation
3. An overview of your company
4. Features of your product or service

If so, you probably wasted valuable time delivering details of little importance while your prospect's old brain was wide awake. Chances are, you didn't get to the core of your message before your audience's old brain switched into idle mode. What a missed opportunity to deliver the highlights of your story to the brain's decision-maker!

Typically, many individuals present the most important content too late in their presentations. Take a product demo as an example: Your demo might contain two or three key desirables that could really change your prospect's life with unique, measurable gain. But if you catch your prospect at a low attention level, he or she will miss the gain entirely. You have lost a valuable opportunity that you can never recapture!

> Make a strong first impression by creating a powerful grabber.

The purpose of using a grabber is to present your gain upfront. Just like mining for gold, your prospects will stay attentive longer if they actually discover several gold nuggets in the first three minutes.

Grabbers have tremendous impact because, as we've all heard before, you only have one chance to make a first impression. As a seller, your first impression needs to be a strong one. The old brain is quick to judge and label; it can immediately recognize and categorize a potential threat. Furthermore, once judgment is passed, it's very difficult for the old brain to change its first impression. Begin your presentation or message with a grabber that is centered around your prospect's most prominent pain, and you'll set the stage for a great start.

You can develop a better understanding of this process by examining the natural "Human Resistance Curve" (Figure 8-2). This curve

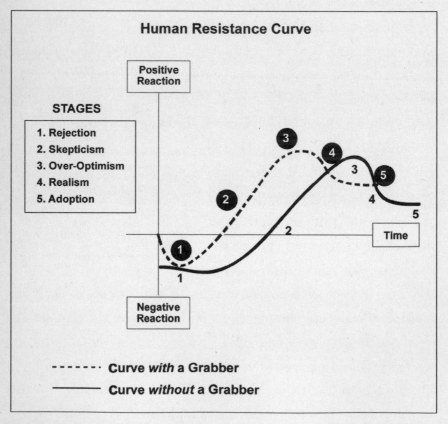

FIGURE 8-2

shows the five natural stages of human reaction to any new idea or message. The solid line represents an average adoption curve that does not have a grabber. The dotted line shows how one adopts the concept more easily and more quickly when one is exposed to a message with a strong grabber.

By using a grabber, you ensure that your prospects will go through the five phases of the Human Resistance Curve much faster. Moreover, their overall reactions will remain more positive in the long run.

In advertising, print ads are frequently just big grabbers: there isn't the time or space to present anything else, so the message has to catch the reader's attention right away. Humor is another type of grabber often used at the beginning of speeches and presentations.

TYPES OF GRABBERS

The best grabbers to reach the old brain can be classified into five specific categories:

1. *Mini-dramas*: describing a painful day in the life of your prospect contrasted with the benefits of your solution.
2. *Wordplays*: utilizing creative language to get attention.
3. *Rhetorical Questions*: letting their brain produce the answer you want.
4. *Props*: using an object that symbolizes what your solution could do for your prospect.
5. *Stories*: sharing a story that will elicit a response from the old brain.

Grabber 1: Mini-dramas

When you sell fire-extinguishers, open with the fire.
~David Ogilvy, Advertising Expert

A mini-drama is basically a reenactment of a "day in the life" of your prospect without the benefit of your product or service. If done well, it will make your prospect relive the pain he daily experiences from not using your product or service.

The most effective mini-dramas close with a second act: a reenactment of the same situation with the benefit of your product or service. A sharp contrast helps the prospect experience the difference, and it stimulates the contrast-sensitive old brain.

Here's an example of a mini-drama a friend of mine, Agnes Perrot, performed during a job interview:

The product: Agnes Perrot, a successful professional with an engineering background and a great personality. She had worked supporting sales engineers with a technology company for the past four years and wanted a job with a higher salary, more responsibility, and some travel.

The prospect: A hot Internet company in the process of expanding its international operations in Latin America. They sought someone based in the San Francisco headquarters to help their distributors with all pre- and post-sales issues. The job required a strong technical background and a capacity to interact with other prospects—in this case, mostly distributors.

The pre-work: Agnes had customized her résumé to fit the job description. She had already been to a first interview with the HR department and to a second interview with the recruiting director. They had told her that she was one of three final candidates for the job.

The problem: Although the interviewers expressed complete confidence in Agnes's technical knowledge, they mentioned some concerns about her sales skills. To dissipate this objection, they asked Agnes to come and give a twenty-minute presentation on the subject of why they should hire her.

The plan: When Agnes called me, she was both excited about the opportunity and scared about the next step of the recruiting process. We met late on a Friday to prepare for her Tuesday appointment.

We first discussed why her potential employer was recruiting—in other words, their pain. She said that they were growing quickly, but their Latin American distributors were complaining about a poor level of responsiveness, a lack of proper communication, some missed commitments due to time difference and language issues, and the inability to get timely and accurate technical responses.

After establishing the pain, we then explored what was unique about Agnes. What could she present to the recruiting people that no other candidate could claim? On the technical side, she already knew that her skills were a great match for the job, so most likely, this would be one of her unique claims.

Agnes was also fluent in Spanish. Although the other candidates might also claim to speak Spanish, Agnes's mastery of the language and her knowledge and understanding of the culture would be another valuable claim.

Next, we discussed how Agnes could prove the gain she could bring to her prospective employer. Agnes had a number of interesting stories from her previous job experience where she really had made a difference. She had helped to close at least two multimillion-dollar deals, so she had a great example to prove her financial value. She also had similar customer stories that would prove her strategic gain as well.

In addition to these gains, Agnes had strong references from her previous management praising her internal responsiveness and technical abilities. These references would demonstrate some personal gain for her future coworkers and customers, since they would not have to worry about getting the wrong answers from her, or worse, no answers at all.

Loaded with all of this information, we at last talked about how Agnes could present with maximum impact. We needed a strong grabber. Agnes had never done a mini-drama before, and even the word "mini-drama" made her feel uncomfortable: she believed she had no talent for acting. However, during the course of our interaction, she gradually became convinced that this particular type of grabber could have huge impact, so she agreed to try.

The presentation: Agnes arrived promptly at her Tuesday appointment, where she was greeted by three people: the VP of sales, the recruiting director, and the HR director. They immediately invited her to begin her presentation.

Ignoring the nearby projector the company had set up in anticipation of a PowerPoint presentation, Agnes said, "Let's take a look at the life of your distributors today. Imagine it's 6:00 p.m. on a Friday, and Marco, your Venezuelan distributor, has a problem with the software. He has an important demo with a large prospect on Monday."

Here, Agnes picks up her portable phone. Speaking in the phone as if she were Marco, she pretends she is desperately trying to reach somebody at the supplier's San Francisco office. After several tries and transfers, Agnes—playing Marco—finally manages to get a live person on the phone.

Marco's English is far from fluent, so Agnes imitates Marco by mixing both Spanish and English as she tries to get her issue solved with the person she has finally reached on the phone.

In the mini-drama, Marco gets disconnected, so Agnes desperately dials again, playing on the frustration and desperation Marcos is experiencing at this point in his interaction with the company. By now it's 6:30 p.m., and when somebody finally picks up the phone, it's a person from the sales department who cannot be of any assistance to Marco. No one in the supplier's office seems to recognize or care that it is now 10:30 p.m. in Caracas, and they are likely going to miss the biggest opportunity yet in Venezuela—all because nobody is available to help Marco.

Finally, having demonstrated Marco's aggravation to a very painful point, Agnes hangs up the call with a grim look on her face, signifying the results of her desperate efforts to find a solution to the problem.

After a dramatic pause, Agnes walked slowly to the other side of the room and said, "Now, let's see what would happen to Marco if you hired somebody like me."

Once again, Agnes picks up her cellular phone, ostensibly dialing from Caracas on a Friday night at 10:00 p.m. local time. Instead of calling the central number at the San Francisco supplier's office, she—still acting as Marco—dials the direct line for Agnes Perrot, the newly hired technical contact for South America.

Agnes, speaking as Marco: "Hello, Agnes, *es Marco de Caracas, ¿cómo estás?*"

Agnes, speaking as herself: "*Muy bien, Marco, ¿y tú?*"

Marco: *"Tengo un problema con el software . . ."*
Agnes: *"Sí entiendo. Es porque . . ."*

Agnes switches her phone from her left hand, signaling Marco, to her right, signaling herself. She also uses a different voice to make it clear when "Marco" is speaking. Occasionally, Agnes blocks the phone with her hand to tell the three people in the room what is happening as she conducts the call in Spanish. She explains to her audience that the deal Marco is working on is for about five hundred licenses, the largest South American contract their company has ever worked on. Speaking to Marco, Agnes even offers to fly to Venezuela to help close the deal. It is obvious to everyone that Marco is having a much better experience now that Agnes is on board.

As the call ends, Marco is evidently very happy with the help and support he has received.

The final act of the drama unfolds when "Marco" calls Agnes back on Monday evening to explain that his demo was such a huge success that the prospect is now talking about placing an order for one thousand licenses. Because of the size of the deal, Marco is requesting the presence of Agnes for the next sales call, where he hopes to close the deal.

After the mini-drama ended and Agnes had "hung up" from the final call, she went back to her seat and asked her audience if they could see how the life of their distributors would be impacted if they were to hire somebody with both her technical and cultural skills.

As you may have noticed, Agnes had chosen her two unique claims as:

- The right technical skills, and
- The right cultural skills.

The whole mini-drama lasted no more than three minutes, and Agnes was eager to move to the next part of her presentation, where she would deliver the proofs of gain of her two claims. However, at this point, something odd happened. The VP of sales interrupted and asked Agnes if she would mind leaving the room for a few minutes so the three could have a private discussion. While she waited, Agnes was nervous: Had she overdone it? Did they feel her acting was unprofessional?

When they called her back a few minutes later, Agnes was prepared to hear the all-too-familiar, "Thank you. We'll let you know next week."

But as Agnes reentered the room, the VP of sales smiled at her warmly, "I have never seen a better demonstration of sales skills. What will it take to bring you on board?" The rest of the interview was focused on the job conditions, salary requirements, and logistics. Agnes was not even asked to finish her presentation. She was offered the position and given a handshake agreement on the spot. In three short minutes, Agnes had managed to convince the three of them that she was the right person for the job.

Agnes called me back about two weeks later, after she signed the letter of employment. She was thrilled about her new job, and she was even more surprised and pleased that they had increased her compensation package over and above what she had requested.

What a testimony to the impact of conveying a message that goes beyond words yet generates an intense emotional response in the brain of your audience! The grabber Agnes used contrasted the customer's pain before interacting with Agnes with the customer's gain after interacting with her. The selling power of such a mini-drama was enough to convince three people at once that she was the best person for the job. It also managed to prove the gain of the claims she was making in three short minutes.

Easy? Yes! And no: the mini-drama took Agnes a complete weekend of brainstorming and several hours of rehearsal. At first, Agnes wasn't entirely comfortable with her planned performance. But, looking back, she now says it was the best possible investment of her time. A mini-drama is the most efficient way of impacting the old brain. It focuses on the pain of the prospect and creates both an emotional reaction and a strong, memorable event.

Panasonic even used a mini-drama in a print ad I came across recently. The ad was for Toughbook computers and proceeded to describe a situation where an individual, rushing to a pending presentation, accidentally dropped his laptop in the street. Reading the ad, I was caught up in the drama of the tale, my heart plunging right along with the computer in the story as it tumbled to the ground. However, wonder of wonders, the laptop was undamaged, and the hero was able to continue on his way with no further problem.

In reality, mini-dramas are entertaining stories that are imbued with emotion. How can you turn a story into a mini-drama? Let's borrow Panasonic's idea for a minute and imagine that you were selling computers with a similar claim to Toughbook's. To make that ad's claim come alive, you could drop the notebook during your presentation, making it seem to be an accident. Then, looking desperate, you could build on the pain by telling your audience that you've probably broken the computer, lost all your data, and you will not be able to continue the presentation.

Once they are hooked, you would make your point about the gain they can experience with your solution by saying something like, "Oh, I forgot; this is a Brand X Indestructa computer, so everything is fine," and simply show that your laptop is still working—a great demo as a proof of value!

GRABBER 2: WORDPLAYS

Wordplays are attention-getters. Good grabbers add another layer of meaning, typically through humor or logic, to the original content of a sentence. As such, they engage the whole brain: new, middle, and old brain.

Here are some examples of some companies' well-used wordplays:

- *More bank for your buck.* In just five words, Wells Fargo Bank emphasizes the fact that they'll offer you the best banking service (claim) for little cost (financial gain).
- *Blue for a better airline?* Jet Blue.
- *When News Gets Broken, Blame Us* ABC News.

Finding good wordplays can be difficult and often requires the assistance of an ad agency. Such grabbers are effective in printed ads and other marketing collateral, where advertisers can use color and design to enhance their wordplay.

GRABBER 3: RHETORICAL QUESTIONS

Because there are no guarantees that your prospect will actually listen to what you are saying, why not start by asking a question designed to engage the brain in seeking an answer which coincides with one of your strong benefits? Rhetorical questions represent an easy, interesting way of providing important information such as numbers, figures, and statistics that otherwise may not be friendly to the old brain.

Here are some good types of rhetorical questions.

1. *"What if you . . . ?" questions*

Imagine you are selling pacemakers to hospitals, and you are making a presentation at a large medical conference. Assume these are the claims you wish to establish about your product: (1) long battery life, (2) small size, and (3) easy installation.

You could start your presentation by saying this:

What if you and your patients could rely on a pacemaker that would last for ten years?
(4-second pause)
What if you could easily hide the device so that it becomes totally invisible?
(4-second pause)
What if you could install it in less than four hours?
(4-second pause)

Do you notice that by asking such questions you draw the reader or listener into an internal dialogue? In fact, your audience will start to think about the positive things that would happen in their lives if they had access to the benefits of your product.

The financially driven doctor will think about how many more pacemakers he can implant monthly; the medically driven doctor will think about the increased autonomy it provides to his patients or how much safer the procedure is; the aesthetically driven doctor will think about the fact that the device is totally invisible.

Using this technique, you are not forcing the functions or features of your product onto the prospects; you are simply enabling them to visualize how the benefits would positively impact their lives.

To make your "What if you . . . ?" questions most effective, it is important to

- Carefully choose the questions to reflect on the benefits of your claims.
- Make the questions simple and short. The rule is to ask a question that is shorter than one normal line of text.
- Pause for at least four seconds at the end of each question. Without a pause, your audience will not have enough time to think about the answer to that question.
- Use "What if you . . . ?" questions to appeal to the personal, self-centered aspect of the old brain.

"What if you . . . ?" questions also have great impact as print ads. W Hotels created one that showed a couple enjoying the comforts of their hotel room and appealed to the emotional side of the old brain, asking, "What if you found true love?" You can't help but think about the gain you might enjoy from any well-crafted "What if you . . . ?" question.

2. "What do these words have in common?" questions

Another effective way to engage the old brain of your audience is to start your presentation by writing down a series of words and asking, "What do these words have in common?"

For example, one of our clients had defined a new paradigm for developing complex software. The main benefit of his solution (an automatic, intelligent, code-generating system) was a dramatic decrease in software development costs: up to seven times less expensive than the existing process.

You would think such a huge savings would yield an instant *yes* from his prospects. However, his prospects systematically underestimated their actual development costs because, at the beginning of a project, they could not predict all the different factors that would impact their bottom line. Since they were consistently unable to foresee how much it would take to complete a given project, they did not understand the gain they would receive by using my client's solution.

To make prospects aware of this issue, my customer used the following grabber:

What do the following have in common?
- Radio waves
- Magnetic fields
- Black holes
- The future
- Hidden software development costs

The answer? Scientific evidence can show that they all exist, even though they are not easily visible.

When their old brain was challenged to make the connection between software development costs and other abstract concepts, the prospects were able to change their perception of how substantial those costs really could be. This paradigm shift allowed them to glimpse what benefits they would derive by using this solution.

3. *"What do these numbers have in common?"* questions

A rhetorical question similar to the previous type of question is called a number play. Sina Fahte, a CEO in the hardware industry, started a presentation to a small group of venture capitalists by asking the following:

What do these numbers have in common?

- 120
- 25
- 10 to 2
- 5 and 3
- 100

After a one-minute pause while the audience analyzed the situation, Sina completed the demonstration by saying, "These numbers represent the state of the wireless market and what we could do for it:

- 120 million is the number of wireless devices sold this year.
- 25 is the annual percentage of growth of this market.
- 10 dollars is the cost of our solution today—reducing to 2 dollars over a 3-year period.
- 5 is the number of granted patents we have already received with 3 more pending.
- Finally, we project that our revenues will grow to 100 million dollars in 5 years."

Typically, those same numbers would be presented in a conventional corporate overview format which, though accepted by the new and middle brain, has little or no impact on the old brain. By using a number play in the form of a question, you make sure that your audience's old brain doesn't fall asleep: it is a fast and effective way of presenting important numbers or words with impact.

We have shown you examples of the different types of targeted questions you as a seller may create and pointed out the value that's found in the rhetorical. As you can see, the "yes" answer you want from your prospects is often just one right question away.

Grabber 4: Props

Most of us love props because they are tangible and visual—they even remind us of toys we had when we were kids. This attachment for simple, concrete objects or props is deeply rooted in our old brain. Interestingly, recent research has proven that objects identified as "tools" have the biggest impact on the old brain. Using a prop in your presentation will ensure that your prospect will remember your message—Guaranteed!

Of course, the object you choose should have powerful significance in the world of your prospect—it is not just mere entertainment. You will want to use a prop when you need your prospect to remember one of the benefits of your solution forever.

Here are some real-life examples of how you could use a prop:

Natasha Deganello is head of Shabono, a firm specializing in corporate identities and branding. One day, one of her prospects called to request a presentation of her portfolio. Her prospect was a mid-sized software company specializing in security software who wanted to redesign their logo, recreate their brochure, and solidify their corporate identity. Natasha had reviewed all the collateral of her prospect and agreed that they needed to standardize their corporate image to make it consistent and cohesive.

Natasha met with the CEO, the VP of marketing, and the director of communication.

"Today, you have three different product lines," she said. "Each one deals with security. The first is a simple security encryption for small network applications. The second is for Web-enabled applications, and the third consists of security products for large e-commerce applications that require commercial grade security. To ensure that the software will not be broken into or stolen, you provide locks."

> Recent research has proven that objects identified as "tools" have the biggest impact on the old brain. Using a prop in your presentation will ensure that your prospect will remember your message—Guaranteed!

Natasha pulled a large lock out of her bag and waved it in front of them as she continued, "The problem, however, is that each of your three divisions designs different locks."

Natasha pulled a second and a third type of lock out of her bag.

"No wonder you have a corporate identity issue," she said smoothly. "You are currently sending several different messages to your prospects, almost to the point of appearing to be several different companies."

She waved the three very different types of locks in front of her executive audience.

"I can help you look like one company, with similar locks, to meet your prospects' broad needs."

With a flourish, she brought out three locks of different sizes but exactly the same model.

Natasha finished the presentation by showing off her portfolio as proofs of gain to her prospect. A few days later, Natasha signed a contract. Per her suggestion, the company started buying small key chains with a lock that they leave behind every time they meet with a prospect.

Here is another example of the lasting impact a prop can have:

Back when I worked at Silicon Graphics, their logo was a 3D cube. In my capacity, I had to give many presentations about the company and their products: supercomputers, large graphics workstations, and servers.

Knowing the value of a good prop, I found an eight-inch cube that looked exactly like the Silicon Graphics logo and used it to explain how the graphics engine inside the machine processed geometrical information. This was a strong claim for SGI, allowing the user to rotate, zoom-in, pan, tilt, or even slice any object in any possible position.

> That's the power of using a prop: people will remember you and your presentation long after the impact of a traditional message normally fades away.

The SGI hardware was very complex, and few people really understood how the "geometry engine" worked. However, 100 percent of my prospects loved the prop because it helped them see how the SGI system worked and why it was unique.

One day, years later, as I walked through the airport in Munich, Germany, a stranger approached me saying, "You're the cube guy! You probably don't remember me, but I visited your headquarters about three years ago with a large group of German executives, and I remember your presentation with the cube. In fact, my company ended up placing a large order for SGI computers."

That's the power of using a prop: people will remember you and your presentation long after the impact of a traditional message normally fades away. That man will forget most everything I said, but the image of the prop and its basic claim will be forever stored in the long-term memory of his brain.

How to Use Props

1. *Use a prop to illustrate a specific point of your presentation—* and make sure it's relevant. At the end of the day, it may be the only thing they remember about you.
2. *Choose a prop that is appropriate in the environment in which you are presenting.* Using a pack of cigarettes as a prop during a lung cancer conference may be a bad idea—or it could get you a standing ovation. It all depends on the context and the audience.
3. *Rehearse.* Just like a joke with a bad punch line, nothing can make you look more foolish than if your prop fails to illustrate your point. Looking back at the woman who used locks as a prop for a presentation to a software security company, imagine the negative connotation to the old brain if one of the locks accidentally popped open while she was using it to demonstrate the security and dependability of the solution!

GRABBER 5: STORIES

*The writer's job is to dig so much into his own story
that he reaches everyone's story.*

I once heard a story originally told by Winston Churchill in the late 1930s. His objective in telling the story was to convince the British Parliament to approve his request for a larger military budget. The increase was necessary to allow the development of new weapons. However, Churchill was facing opposition by a number of representatives who strongly rejected the idea of increasing the budget for new, unproven technologies. He told the story of the battle of Om-Duram as follows:

Remember the war England fought in Africa in the late 1800s? Our troops were fighting the Whirling Dervishes. The Dervishes were strong and courageous soldiers, and although their only weapons were swords, we suffered heavy losses. We had only one-shot guns back then.

Just imagine what it was like for one of our soldiers to fight that war; you've been in the desert for four months, and after yet another poor night of sleep, you wake up with a dry mouth and a burning thirst. It's going to be very hot again today, and you are craving a good cup of tea. As the sun rises, you anxiously await a new wave of attacks by the Dervishes. You are hiding out in six-foot trenches, and the still air signifies a terrifying calm before the storm. The sun is turning the purple horizon into deep blood-red, and you can't escape the memory of yesterday's battle where you lost three friends to violent deaths.

Suddenly, in the distance, you see those terrifying red turbans. As the battle begins, you panic during the endless twenty seconds it takes to reload your gun after each shot. That delay gives the Dervishes and their curved swords plenty of time to approach. By now, you have calculated your odds, and you know that for every Dervish that will die today, a British soldier will have to give his life.

This was the horrific reality of war until October 21, 1898. On that day, everything changed. Britain provided troops with the newly introduced Gatlin gun, the first automatic weapon. It could fire hundreds of shots per minute. Thanks to the Gatlin gun, during the final battle of Om-Duram, only 48 British soldiers died when 10,000 Dervishes lay dead, 16,000 wounded, and 5,000 were made prisoners.

And that's the benefit of keeping up with technology or thinking it will always be the same.

(Story based on sources: *Death Before Dishonour*, 1982; *Toll of the Brave*, 1963; *Hector Macdonald: His Rise Through the Ranks and His Contributions to the British Empire*, 1980; *My Early Life: W. S. Churchill*, 1930.)

After Churchill's story, the Parliament voted overwhelmingly to approve his proposal.

Now if you had been a British soldier fighting that war, would you be for or against an increased budget to develop new weapons? Most likely you would be for it because it would have saved your life.

The impact of a good story is that it makes your old brain

believe that you have actually lived it. Stories put the audience in a world of sensory impressions that make it impossible for the old brain to differentiate between the reality and the story: the old brain feels that it has lived through the experience even if it has only heard it.

What else makes stories so appealing to the old brain? Can stories actually increase your ability to sell to the old brain? Let's look at stories from another perspective.

What do the following people have in common?
• Parents
• Grandparents
• Relatives
• Friends
• Spiritual leaders

Answer: They all care about us, and they have all told us stories at one time or another.

That's why, whenever you tell a story, the subliminal message is that you care for your audience. It opens up their old brain to your message.

Think of it this way: Let's imagine that I am one of your colleagues, sent into your office to pick up a document on Monday morning. If I don't know you personally, it is highly unlikely that either of us will tell the other a story about what we did over the weekend. However, if we were friends, it is natural that we would feel comfortable relaying a detailed account of our respective weekends. Stories equal caring.

All leaders have the ability to tell stories that motivate people to act. In *Leadership in Paradoxical Age*, author Noel Tichy rates the art of storytelling as the number three criterion that makes leaders, third only to taking responsibility for the leadership training of others and developing teachable points of view in the areas of ideas, values, and emotional energy.

Stories represent a powerful way of highlighting one of your benefits or one of your claims. They help you make a point without resistance or objections from your audience.

Do you remember the story of Agnes Perrot's job interview and how she conducted a mini-drama to create impact?

Stories can come from any source, as long as you can tie them into the world of your prospect. They are a subtle but strong way to imprint an idea on the mind of your listener. Imagine the impact if that very imprinted idea is one of your claims.

Unfortunately, telling stories is an art in which many business people have not been trained. Here are a few tips that make for good stories:

1. Be sure that your story has a point, and be sure you make the connection for your audience. Don't rely on them to draw the connection on their own. A story with no point is like a joke with no punch line—it's a waste of time.
2. Make the story personal. Don't say, "A woman went to a job interview." Say "Agnes went to a job interview."
3. Put passion into your story. Add details that prove you really lived or experienced that story. Create those sensory impressions that will impact the old brain and help your prospects envision themselves in the story.

An effective way to use a story with a prospect is to tell a customer story. If you were presenting to Mercedes, for example, imagine the impact of using a story that illustrates what BMW gained by using your solution.

When telling a customer story, be sure to:

- *Include the company name* if confidentiality is not an issue. Also include the name of the key person who is featured in the story. This makes it more tangible for your listener.
- *Make it personal.* Draw at least three parallels between the prospect in the story and the company you are presenting to.
- *Contrast* what your prospect's life was like before your product with their life after they started using your product.
- *Present specific, tangible benefits* instead of using generalities.
- *Highlight the gain*: financial, strategic, or personal.

You can never overestimate the power of a meaningful, well-told story. In fact, stories are so important that we will discuss them again later in this book.

WHAT TO REMEMBER

It is crucial to speak to your prospects' old brain at both the beginning and end of your presentation. Use a strong grabber to jump-start your presentation and wow your audience early, when they are still attentive. Grabbers include any of the following techniques:

- A mini-drama to generate strong emotions
- A wordplay to force your audience to think about the benefits of your solution in a creative, sometimes fun, way
- A rhetorical question to convey important numbers or information without putting your audience to sleep
- A prop to make sure they will remember your point . . . forever
- A story to influence your audience without appearing pushy or even showing that you are selling

MESSAGE BUILDING BLOCK #2: BIG PICTURE

A picture is worth a thousand words.

~UNKNOWN

An enormous body of research, particularly that of Dr. Joseph LeDoux, director of neuroscience at New York City University, has shown that, of all our senses, the visual input reaches the old brain fastest. In fact, neuroscientists have demonstrated that the old brain registers images long before the new one can recognize or analyze them. As described in chapter 2, Ledoux demonstrated that your old brain would typically make you react in about two milliseconds (two-thousandths of a second) to the sight of a snake. Yet it would take a full 500 milliseconds—250 times longer—before you would consciously recognize that what you've seen is a snake.

Technically, visual stimuli follow two simultaneous paths in the brain before reaching the visual cortex, an area located in back of the new brain. One path, known as the "low path," traverses the old brain to reach the visual cortex, while the second path, the "high path," remains in the new brain.

A very rare condition exists known as "blind vision." In this state, neurons on the visual path in a person's new brain have been damaged, rendering them blind. But even though the patient cannot consciously recognize an object, he or she can still detect its existence or movement, as processed by the survival-oriented old brain.

Topping off all this information is the fact that the visual nerve carries information forty times faster than the auditory nerve. So what is the best way to add a visual component to your message so it goes directly to the decision-maker, your prospect's old brain? A Big Picture.

GETTING IT AT A GLANCE

A big picture is a visual or graphical representation of how your solution can impact the world of your prospect. Often people use graphs or images, which they mistakenly believe are big pictures.

The two reasons most images or pictures are *not* big pictures are:

1. They do not reflect the world of the prospect.
A good example of a picture that does not reflect its audience is an airline's famous map showing its worldwide connections, often found

in their in-flight magazine. The map is not a big picture because it mostly centers on the world of the airline, not the world of the traveler. Indeed, as a traveler, other than minimizing your travel time, why would you care about where your airline connects?—It's their world not yours! In contrast, the following Canadian Airline ad (Figure 9-1) truly shows your world.

2. They are not real visuals.

How many typical block diagrams have you seen with squares, arrows, circles, and text within a box? Many people think these diagrams are visual information, but they are not. They cannot be processed in a mode that triggers a real visual processing response, and thus are not big pictures.

Now take a look at an airline who understood the big picture. Canadian Airlines discovered that one of the main areas of pain for their business travelers was the fact that the batteries on their portable computers typically ran out after one or two hours of run-time—consequently wasting valuable working time during long flights (Figure 9-1).

This ad qualifies as a big picture because it's a simple representation of how the airline's solution—a power plug for laptops—will impact the world of their prospects: Even if you fall asleep, in a Canadian Airlines' airplane, your computer will not run out of power.

Big pictures are very important. As visual stimuli, they go directly to the old brain. They also provide a canvas for the more detailed information you may provide later, accelerating the understanding of complex concepts.

we believe your laptop

should always last the length of your flight

and we go to hong kong

FIGURE 9-1

CONTRASTED BIG PICTURES

Even more effective, contrasted big pictures consist of two images: first, the life of the prospect is shown without your product or service, and then it is shown with the benefit of your product or service. The first picture should clearly emphasize the pain, while the second one illustrates the relief of the pain through your product or solution.

We have all seen those traditional "Before and After" print ads with an overweight person on the left side and a picture of the same person weeks or months later after he or she has lost fifty pounds. Or the similar contrasted big pictures with balding men on the left side who display a full head of hair on the right side. This type of big picture—before/after, without/with—uses an extremely effective visual contrast that directly impacts the old brain.

Remember that the old brain prefers contrast so it can make a good decision quickly and easily. In a well-contrasted ad (Figure 9-2), Microsoft shows you the pain on the left side of the ad and the gain (or relief) on the right side. Note how the visual contrast of the two images immediately enables you to understand the benefit of the solution regardless of how sophisticated or complex the product actually is.

In another example of a contrasted big picture (Figure 9-3), notice how a fishing analogy is used to represent the world of recruiters. What if you were a recruiter looking for a very specific type of candidate? In this big picture, if you were specifically trying to catch a Red-Spotted Grouper fish, in which location would you rather fish? Does this ad illustrate the contrast of your world both with and without Careerbuilder? Can you feel the underlying pain of the individual

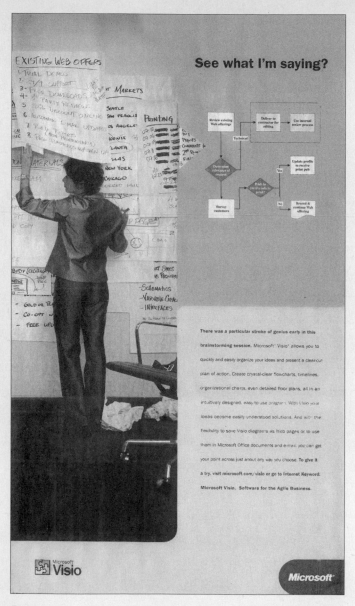

FIGURE 9-2   PHOTOGRAPHY BY GARRY OWNES / CPI

FIGURE 9-3

fishing in the ocean? How long did it take you to understand the gain offered by Careerbuilder?

To maximize your impact, it is more effective to show the pain first and to portray the relief after. This is why, for Western societies, the "before" or "without" image is usually on the left or top, and the "after" or "with" scenario is normally placed on the right or the bottom. In other cultures, where the normal reading pattern is from right to left, the order should be changed accordingly.

Along with grabbers, giving your prospects the big picture helps to gain maximum attention from the old brain. Remember, the old brain is visual and cannot easily be influenced by words. Allowing your prospects to visualize the benefits of your solution is an excellent way to enhance understanding in their old brain.

WHAT TO REMEMBER

The Second Message Building Block you need from the Selling to the Old Brain toolbox is a Big Picture. Delivering a big picture helps your prospect visualize the benefits of your solution. Big pictures are graphical representations of how your solution can impact their world—not block diagrams of your system! Even more effective, a contrasted big picture shows the prospect what his life would be like before/after your product or without/with it. Be sure to show the prospect's pain first, and then the relief gained by your solution.

MESSAGE BUILDING BLOCK #3: CLAIMS

If you have an important point to make, don't be subtle or clever. Use a pile driver. Hit the point once. Then hit it again. Then hit it a third time—a tremendous whack.

~WINSTON CHURCHILL, FORMER BRITISH PRIME MINISTER

When you give a presentation or message in any form, it is vital that your prospects leave with a solid understanding of your claims. What, then, are claims exactly? Claims are your key selling points; they represent the actual value of your solution. For the sake of analogy, if your product or service were a story, your claims would be the titles of the story chapters—the headings under which you organize your proofs of gain.

In essence, your claims are the top reasons why your prospects should buy from you.

To help your prospects remember your claims, you need to make them both short and relevant. Clear, focused claims will help your prospects retain your core message, and if they are short, you will satisfy the old brain's bias for tangible and simple information. As you share your claims, also be sure to include several absolute proofs that show the gain that each of your claims will provide.

> Make your claims more memorable by repeating them again and again.

Repeat your claims frequently throughout your message. Even the repetition of a few simple words sends a strong signal to the old brain, prompting it to note, "I should remember that." Once your prospects are able to memorize and repeat your claims consistently and accurately to other members both inside and outside the organization, they will become your best active promoters and supporters. Such an effective selling of your unique claims will naturally disqualify your competitors.

FOOL-PROOFING YOUR CLAIMS

1. *Edit your claims* to make them the shortest and simplest possible. This really makes it easy for your prospect to remember them.
2. *Keep your claims relevant* to your prospect; be sure they provide a cure to your prospect's pain.
3. *Repeat your claims* so that the old brain will bookmark them as important.

COMMUNICATE YOUR CLAIMS

Once you have come up with clear, concise claims that address your prospects' pain, how do you communicate those claims? In a conversation or presentation, you can signal your listeners that a claim is coming up by using phrases like, "The only thing you need to remember is . . . ," "Let me repeat . . . ," or "It all comes down to . . . ."

> To make them memorable, wordsmith your claims to be the shortest and simplest possible.

Not too long ago, Sprint PCS ran a print ad featuring a crystal image of a map of the United States with a cell phone engraved into the middle. The words "Free and Clear" were repeated four separate times on the one-page ad, and the entire value proposition was developed around these two claims:

Free: you pay no roaming charges (a financial value)
Clear: you get a crystal clear connection (a personal value)

In the next ad (Figure 10-1), Nationwide promotes three memorable claims: *Speed, Simplicity, Savings*. Notice how they develop the value proposition under each one of those three claims, and how they repeat all three claims several times on the page to help the old brain to remember them.

Next, in a full-page ad published in a San Francisco newspaper (Figure 10-2), "graffiti" is cleverly used to highlight the claims. Although it is always preferable to repeat your claims if time and space

Now you can feel

right at home

about getting a mortgage!

Whether you're a first-time homebuyer, you're ready to refinance, or you're shopping for your next home, Nationwide Advantage Mortgage℠ Company introduces a whole new way to finance your dreams. We're making mortgages fast and easy with our 10-minute mortgage approval. It's just one more way Nationwide is on your side.

What makes Nationwide Advantage Mortgage different from the rest? Take a look:

SPEED
Final approvals in minutes.
Unlike many other lenders who may pre-approve you quickly, but then put you through a lengthy final approval process, we make approvals quick and easy. Whether you submit your application online or by phone, you could have your approval decision in as little as 10 minutes!

SIMPLICITY
One approval includes different options.
You're also going to feel relaxed and right at home because we're not going to ask you to tell your life story. Our short application is surprisingly simple to save you time. We're also different from the rest in another important way. Most lenders will not even start the approval process until you decide on a type of loan. As a Nationwide customer, your approval comes with a list of all the products you have qualified for. So you only apply once, and then enjoy the flexibility of choosing from a variety of real loan options.

SAVINGS
Reduced or eliminated fees.
Compare us to other lenders and you'll find we've reduced or completely eliminated many of the typical costs associated with getting a mortgage. Many of our customers benefit from reduced closing costs like lower appraisal fees. Plus, with Nationwide you won't pay an origination fee!

If you have any questions, expert help is always just a phone call away. From approval through closing, count on the support of an experienced Nationwide Advantage Mortgage loan professional. We're here to answer any questions you have about the mortgage process, and we promise to make buying a new home or refinancing your current one easier than you ever thought possible.

SPEED. SIMPLICITY. SAVINGS.
That's the Nationwide Advantage.

Visit us online anytime at
NationwideAdvantage.com

Or call 1-888-244-8055
Monday through Friday, 7:00 a.m. - 10:00 p.m. ET
or Saturday, 9:30 a.m. - 6:00 p.m. ET

Nationwide
Advantage Mortgage℠

The Nationwide Advantage Mortgage solution is powered by Fannie Mae technology.

Speed. Simplicity. Savings.

FIGURE 10-1

allow, the emphasis from the circles immediately leads you to understand the CarsDirect value proposition:

- Save time (personal gain)
- Save money (financial gain)
- Get the car (strategic gain)

Obviously, CarsDirect had identified these as the three main frustrations of car buyers. The ad also focuses on the pain by reenacting the often drawn-out process of buying a new car. It also appeals to readers as a story because it begins with the words, "Once upon a time . . ."

FIGURE 10-2

All three of these ads made a conscious effort to create easily memorable headlines. Their creators knew, as we have discussed, that a message without claims is like a book without chapters. You cannot overemphasize the importance of strong claims.

CAN YOU NAME OUR CLAIMS?

Quiz time! Can you identify the claims of this book?

How about the Four Steps?

- *Diagnose the pain.* The book guides you in the process of assessing the customer frustrations that are most relevant when they make buying decisions.
- *Differentiate your claims.* The book helps you recognize the importance of selecting up to three differentiators that are critical to the pain, unique, and credible.
- *Demonstrate the gain.* The book tells you how to prove the value with the highest proofs.
- *Deliver to the old brain.* The book teaches you how to create compelling and memorable messages.

From a mnemonic standpoint, notice how each claim starts with a *D* and rhymes with the others. This makes them easier for your old brain to remember. If you have multiple claims, it is typically in your best interest to narrow them to three. Research shows that humans remember information more easily when it comes in sets of three, so your claims will be more memorable if you follow this advice. By using more than that, you may lessen what your customers will remember. After all, "he who emphasizes everything, emphasizes nothing."

But wait a minute. You may have noticed that we have broken our own rule by using four claims instead of a maximum of three, as we suggested. Why? Due to the length of our format—the book—and the amount of time we have to present our claims in detail, we feel comfortable having one additional claim: we have the time and space to use grabbers and visual images to back up our claims and keep your old brain active and involved.

Your message should be constructed in the same manner: Bullet-point your claims, and then build your presentation and proof for each one of them using a grabber, stories, and proofs of gain.

Just as we did when writing this book, you will ultimately have to decide how to best demonstrate the gain to your prospects using the time and methods you have at your disposal, and then how to customize your own claims to your target audience. Your well-crafted and communicated claims, boosted by the Impact Boosters we will teach you, will keep your listener's old brain awake and interested.

What to Remember

Claims are the reasons why the prospect should buy your product; they are your key selling points. Use a maximum of three claims, and keep them short and easy to remember. Organize all your points under these three claims, and repeat them often throughout your message.

MESSAGE BUILDING BLOCK #4: PROOFS OF GAIN

Price is what you pay. Value is what you get.
~Warren Buffett, American Entrepreneur

Note: Since we discussed this subject in length in chapter 6, this chapter will be a brief review. Please refer back to that chapter for more details.

It's 4:45 p.m. in the boardroom. You have presented your grabber, your big picture, and your claims.

Now what do you do? Launch into an emotionally charged sales pitch based on all you've said so far?

Of course not.

After all, who wants to make a financial investment based solely on faith?

It is time to review the core of your message—your proofs. In fact, delivering tangible proofs of the gain is where you should spend 70 percent of your selling effort.

Remember, your old brain is very self-centered, so it only cares about its own benefit, and it's going to be looking for some solid, tangible proof to bring it home with impact.

You don't want to waste your prospects' time by telling them something that holds no value for them, by sharing something with no concrete evidence to support your gain. So after presenting your grabber, big picture, and your claims, you need to back it all up with proofs. By communicating the type of gain you offer to your prospects—financial, strategic, or personal—and the type of proof you intend to use to illustrate it, you will have maximum impact on the old brain.

As we have already discussed, the best proof of gain is a customer story—either a testimonial or a case study—followed respectively, in declining strength, by a demonstration, use of data, and last, by a description of a vision.

> Delivering tangible proofs of the gain is where you should spend 70 percent of your selling effort.

Regardless of what technique you use to prove your gain, your objective should always be to demonstrate the largest amount of gain, present the strongest proof, and creatively deliver the proof so it reaches the old brain with impact. You do this by building compelling value matrices that support your claims.

Proof of GAIN Matrix for Your CLAIMS				
Proof Gain	Customer Story	Demo	Data	Vision
Financial				
Strategic				
Personal				

FIGURE 11-1

BUILDING COMPELLING VALUE MATRICES

For each claim you entered into the worksheet, you need to build a proof of value matrix with the strongest possible proofs. Here is how to do that:

1. Find a customer story that would prove the benefit of your claim. Be prepared to provide precise information such as:
   • The name of the company, with one or two names of key company people who will be willing to relate their high satisfaction with your product or service solution (Your prospect may be skeptical of your claim and may decide to call these references.)

- Three common points between the customer in your story and the prospect listening to your presentation
- A specific problem the customer was able to solve using your solution
- Before/after: what the customer did before and what they gained after using your solution.

2. If you can't find a customer story, can you prove the benefit of your claim with a demo? Be prepared to address these points:
   - Will showing them your product be enough to prove your point?
   - Can you really show them a visible proof? Is it a "hands-on" demo, or does it require conceptual extrapolation?
   - Can you do an A/B comparison demo, where A would show the products of one of your competitors and B would be your products? The prospect should clearly be shown why B (your solution) is better, faster, or cheaper.

3. If a demo isn't possible, do you have data to prove the benefit of your claim?
   - Do you have marketing or statistical data that can prove your benefit? For example, can you prove that by using your product, your prospect would save, say, 10 percent of a no-value-added, time-consuming task? Once that concept is accepted, it will be easier to attach a concrete financial savings to that 10 percent of time saved.

4. If none of the above is available, how can you use a vision to prove your benefit?
  • Can you use a story, analogy, or metaphor to best prove why you believe your prospect would receive some benefit by buying from you?

So your objective at this stage is really to demonstrate to your prospect that the value they will receive is greater than their cost. Why would they buy if they'd receive a negative gain? Their gain can be defined as the sum of the value of each of your claims minus your cost:

$$\text{Gain} = \text{Value Claim 1} + \text{Value Claim 2} + \text{Value Claim 3} = \text{Cost}$$

And remember that in this equation you should include the financial, strategic, and personal dimension of the value and cost.

Once you have mastered the concept of showing your proof of gain effectively, you only need two more Message Building Blocks in order to deliver a powerful selling message.

However, though all the building blocks we have shared are important, proofs of gain are the most critical part of your message. If you cannot reasonably prove the measurement of a benefit, FIND ANOTHER CLAIM!

WHAT TO REMEMBER

For each claim, you must find a proof for each benefit and make a strong effort to communicate that proof in such a way that it becomes easy and fast for your prospect to "believe" what you say. The burden of proof is always on you, not on your customers.

MESSAGE BUILDING BLOCK #5:
HANDLING OBJECTIONS

An objection is not a rejection;
it is simply a request for more information.
~Bo Bennett, Author

Handling objections is a favorite topic in sales training. The objective is always to keep a positive connection with the prospects while still addressing their concerns. Objections should be addressed from the viewpoint of the true decision-maker, the old brain.

Objections fall into two categories:

1. Misunderstandings
2. Valid objections

Handling Objections
Resulting from Misunderstandings

Objections are often not rooted in logic. Instead, they are the visible evidence of how your prospect perceives you, your product, and your company. Imagine you are selling computer systems and you've done everything right: you've diagnosed the pain, differentiated your claims, and demonstrated your proofs of gain in a solid presentation using a fantastic grabber, a big picture, and claims. Your selling effectiveness is off the charts, and you're sure your prospect's old brain is completely convinced.

However, just as you reach the end of your sales cycle, your prospect announces that although he is intrigued by your solution, he feels that the speed of the system you offer is not on par with some of your competitors. He insinuates that the level of performance would probably be within the acceptable range of their requirements, but that a faster solution would be more beneficial to their productivity and bottom line. The actual truth is that your system is as fast as any of your top competitors, but somewhere, somehow, the information was either not conveyed or misunderstood. Such objections can typically be handled on a rational level by addressing the new brain. Here's how:

Step 1: *Restate the Objection*
Make sure that you understand the exact nature of the objection by paraphrasing your prospect's comment and openly asking, "Is this your concern?"

In the example you could ask: "It seems like you need a system that provides a certain level of performance. Is speed your concern?"

Step 2: *Step into the Objection*

Your prospect's old brain senses every symptom of fear you portray, however miniscule, especially if you show it in your body language. In fact, communication experts estimate that 55 percent of your impact comes from your body language. When faced with something our old brain perceives as negative or threatening, such as an objection from a prospect, our natural inclination is to move away from the source of the threat. By moving toward rather than away from the person making the objection, you send a very strong message to their old brain: you are not afraid of the objection. As far as your prospect's old brain is concerned, your forward movement will be more important than anything you say.

Step 3: *Hear Your Prospect Out*

Once you've stepped toward your prospect and acknowledged his objection, let him talk. Suspend judgment and practice true listening. As they say, "perception is reality," so if your prospect believes he is right, then he is, and you'll need to understand his point of view before you will overcome his objection.

Step 4: *Deliver the Proof*

Once your prospect has expressed his opinion, it is your turn to calmly and tangibly demonstrate your point of view. In the example above, you must show that the speed of the system you are selling is similar to or better than your competitors'.

Tell a story, offer a customer testimonial, conduct a demo, or present the result of an independent benchmark or a matrix where you report the performance level of your main competitors. When you close on the objection, openly ask your prospect, "Did that help resolve your concern?"

The key in handling objections is to deliver a strong proof of your point of view in a manner the old brain will relate to without discrediting the prospect in the process.

HANDLING VALID OBJECTIONS

Valid objections are caused by your prospect's old brain. They are triggered by the fear of making a wrong decision. Bringing up objections is typically the last step in the buying process. Therefore, you should welcome objections as a sign that your prospect is getting ready to make a purchasing decision. Unfortunately, objections also signal that the proofs of gain you delivered were not strong enough and that your prospect's old brain needs concrete reassurance that it will make a safe choice.

Let's take a look at a very common example of a valid objection: "The price is too high."

The expense of a product is relative, of course. We all want to pay less money for what we own or use, but in reality, we do not always choose to buy the cheapest product.

For example, do you own the cheapest car, the cheapest TV, and the cheapest shoes you could find when you made the decision to buy? Most likely, you did not buy the cheapest option in every one of those cases; you probably bought the item that you needed and that provided you enough proof of the gain you would get from purchasing it.

So, if your prospect objects to your price, you should:

1. Make sure you have fully uncovered your value proposition or gain.
2. Revisit your proofs and make sure they are stronger, more valuable, more tangible, and more personal.

Most often though, using pure logic to handle these objections is not enough. The old brain is not purely rational, and its reactions are based on fear, a highly emotional concept. Here is the most effective way to diffuse a valid objection: reframe it. Do this by beginning with the same three steps you would follow with a misunderstanding.

Step 1: *Restate the objection*

As with an objection related to a misunderstanding, and to avoid further confusion, make sure that you heard the objection correctly. Simply paraphrase your prospect and ask if this is his concern. For example, if your prospect objects to the price, you could say, "It seems that you need a system that will meet some strict financial objectives. Is this your concern?"

Step 2: *Step into the objection*

Again, because the old brain is so sensitive to fear, by moving forward you strongly signal that you are not afraid of the objection. It is necessary that this forward movement occur just after you hear the objection for the first time and as you restate your understanding of the objection.

Step 3: *Wait for their feedback*

Again, both to reassure your prospect and to make sure that you are in tune with his concerns, it is important to listen to what the prospect is saying. Listen to understand so that you will be better able to address his specific worry.

Step 4: *State your personal opinion*

Because these objections have a lot to do with perception, you cannot offer proof as you did with the misunderstanding. Instead, agree or disagree with the objection by simply stating your own opinion. For example, if the objection is about price, you could say: "I understand that your concern at this point is about our pricing. Personally, I find that our prices are very competitive considering the value we offer."

Because the old brain is self-centered, by stating your personal opinion, you make an old brain to old brain connection. You use the power of your credibility to convince your prospect to see your point of view from a new perspective. This is a good way to frame an objection, and although it is not usually enough to dissolve the objection entirely, it will help engage your prospect's old brain.

Step 5: *Present a positive side to the objection*

Most valid objections have a positive side. For example, higher prices often translate to higher quality; late to market means that when the product is finally ready, it will be more robust; old technology often signifies familiarity; and a slower product can mean a more secure solution. Whatever the objection, find the positive side that best counteracts it. Then, the key is to present that unique benefit so it goes directly to the old brain. Remember, using a purely rational approach will not work. The best way is to tell your prospect a story, an analogy, or a metaphor that highlights the importance of the flip side of his objection.

In the "price is too high" example, you could tell your prospect the following story:

"That reminds me of a friend who needed a heart pacemaker and had to choose between two options: going to San Francisco State Hospital where he could receive a good pacemaker for about $5,000 or selecting Stanford Hospital where, for $10,000 more, he would receive the latest, most technologically advanced pacemaker which would be implanted by the best heart surgeon in the nation. Which one do you think he chose?

"Although you might find that our solution is a bit more expensive, we will give you the peace of mind

> Reframe an objection by presenting a positive side to it.

of the most solid, reliable solution to your problem. When the health of your business is at stake, would you want to take any chances?"

If you counter an objection with a story or example, it doesn't necessarily mean that you will overcome that objection immediately or that your prospect will magically change his mind and buy your solution on the spot. If his objection was that the price was too high, most likely he will continue to assume he can find a cheaper solution. But by giving him a snapshot of the proof of gain, you offer a higher quality, risk-free solution—his old brain will begin to weigh your solution against the risk of an unknown or yet-to-be-discovered solution.

Since the unknown does affect the "survival" part of the brain, his old brain will consider your offer very seriously. Your story will slowly but steadily work toward diffusing the objection.

In addition to memorizing the steps for handling objections, keep an ongoing list of the most common objections you receive on a day-to-day basis when you give a presentation or talk about your product or service. Because it is hard to reframe every objection, and because it might take you a while to find a story that perfectly diffuses the objection, prepare a script for each of the main objections and practice delivering and fine-tuning it to achieve the best results.

The most important thing to remember about handling objections is that if you're put on the spot and can't come up with a good response, be sure and remember to move forward when you hear an objection. Your body language does speak louder than your words.

WHAT TO REMEMBER

Misunderstandings and valid objections are a normal and expected part of the sales process, especially when proofs of gain were not communicated as clearly as possible. To handle them effectively, make sure you understand the concern, and then reframe it. Logic alone will not influence your prospect; to reach their old brain, use a story, analogy, or metaphor that highlights the positive side of the objection. Above all else, make sure your positive body language (moving toward the one who objects) conveys calm confidence and respect.

MESSAGE BUILDING BLOCK #6: THE CLOSE

One does not leave a convivial party before closing time.
~Winston Churchill,
Former British Prime Minister

Many sales books suggest a variety of calculated closing techniques. If you have faithfully followed the Four Steps and have designed your message to impact the old brain, there is no need for sophisticated closing techniques. It will be natural for your prospects to buy from you. After all:

- Your prospect will have confirmed the source and intensity of the pain.
- You will have differentiated your claims to show how your solution offers unique relief.
- You will have demonstrated that the value they receive from your claims is greater than your cost: their gain is positive.
- You will have impacted the true decision-maker, the old brain.

Armed with that knowledge, your closing does not have to be a high-pressured do-or-die situation. And yet you also know that the old brain pays particular attention to the bookends of a presentation. Therefore, the most effective closing technique for the old brain is simply to do as follows:

- *Repeat your claims one final time.* "In conclusion, we are the only company who guarantees you will:
  - Save time . . .
  - Save money . . .
  - Get the car . . ."

Again, the old brain remembers the beginning and end. This final repetition reminds the old brain what is important that should be retained.

- *Ask for positive public feedback.* "What do you think?"
- *Ask for the next step.* "Where do we go from here?"

POSITIVE PUBLIC FEEDBACK

To get positive public feedback, simply ask, "What do you think?" and then wait for an answer. If you have a large audience, you can direct the question to one individual.

Why does positive public feedback work? A responding person will want to remain consistent with any public statements he or she made, and will later try to defend his or her initial positive position about you or your product. Several researchers, including successful author and Arizona State University professor Dr. Robert Cialdini, have demonstrated how making a small commitment first triggers a larger commitment.

In a memorable study published in *The Psychology of Persuasion*, Dr. Cialdini selected two identical neighborhoods to conduct an experiment. In neighborhood A, a select sample of households were asked if they would be willing to display a 6' x 8' billboard in their front yard in exchange for one hundred dollars per month. About 1 percent of the households said yes.

In neighborhood B, the same number of households were asked if they would be willing to display a postcard version of the billboard in their front window in exchange for

> Repeat your claims and then get positive public feedback to close.

ten dollars per month. Thirty percent of the households agreed.

Several months later, in Neighborhood B, people who had agreed to display the "postcard" were asked if they would be willing to display the 6' x 8' billboard for exactly the same deal that was originally offered to Neighborhood A.

A full 25 percent of Neighborhood B, the "postcard" group, agreed to display the large billboard in their yard. That means 25 percent of 30 percent, or 7.5 percent, agreed to display the billboard—a number that was 7.5 times more than the initial results from Neighborhood A.

As Dr. Cialdini's experiment shows, it is easier for people to make a bigger commitment toward something if they have first made a smaller commitment. This is called the Law of Consistency—that is, once someone has made a first step in a particular direction, his or her old brain will want to remain consistent with their original decision.

So, your objective when you are asking your audience, "What do you think?" is to compel them to say something positive about your solution. If they do, it will be easier for them to take the next step toward a bigger commitment—like sending you a purchase order!

And if the first comments you hear are not positive? Then you have been given the opportunity to address the objection in public. Chances are, anyone who feels negative for any reason will talk about it with others when you are not around and not present to overcome the objection. Wouldn't you rather try to address and reframe their concerns in person rather than have key questions about your product answered later at the company water cooler? Sometimes entire sales are lost because the presenter did not explicitly address objections and assumptions when given the chance.

Finally, once you have addressed everyone's questions and concerns, it is time to ask, "Where do we go from here?" Again, be patient; let the prospect commit. The key to triggering the Law of Consistency in your audience is not to simply ask for their feedback but to actually wait for it. If your prospect or audience doesn't immediately volunteer their feedback, just pause and wait. Your prospect's suggestion of, "I guess we need to send you a team of three people to further evaluate your solution," is totally different (and more positive) than if you suggest it.

Thanks to the Law of Consistency, if this kind of commitment comes from your prospect, that person becomes personally committed to making that meeting happen. At that point, your prospect or supporter will do whatever he or she can to assemble the team of three people and make sure they perform the evaluation.

WHAT TO REMEMBER

If you have followed the Selling to the Old Brain steps, the close is a natural conclusion to your presentation, not a make-or-break, do-or-die finale. To close effectively, simply

- Repeat your claims one final time.
- Trigger the audience's Law of Consistency by asking: "What do you think?" and then wait.
- Trigger the Law of Consistency again by asking: "Where do we go from here?" and then wait for the prospect's commitment to the next step.

WHAT TO REMEMBER ABOUT THE SIX MESSAGE BUILDING BLOCKS

Each of the Six Message Building Blocks has a specific effect on the old brain. Let's review them once more:

1. **Grabber:** Catch their attention early by introducing compelling cures to their pains.
2. **Big Picture:** Satisfy their old brain with a strong visual stimuli.
3. **Claims:** Repeat the unique reasons your prospects should buy from you.
4. **Proofs of Gain:** Provide irrefutable evidences of the value prospects will gain from you.
5. **Handling Objections:** Dissolve the root of the objection with a story, an analogy, or a metaphor.
6. **Close:** Ask for Positive Public Feedback, and let your prospects commit to the next steps.

THE FIRST
IMPACT BOOSTER:
WORDING WITH "YOU"

A gossip is one who talks to you about others; a bore is one who talks to you about himself; and a brilliant conversationalist is one who talks to you about yourself.

~LISA KIRK, AMERICAN BOOK PUBLICIST

As we mentioned back in chapter 7, you can further boost the impact of each of the Message Building Blocks so they reach the old brain even faster. Think of it this way: if the Message Building Blocks are the dishes on a restaurant menu, the Impact Boosters are the spices you sprinkle on any or all of them to make them more appealing.

Let's now look at the first of the seven techniques that can significantly enhance any and all of your Message Building Blocks.

Impact Booster #1: Wording with "You"

You know the old saying, "The way to a man's heart is through his stomach"? Well, the way to the old brain is through the use of the word *you*.

The fact that the old brain is self-centered and egotistical means your prospects don't care about your products. They only care about what your products can do for them. So, the best way you can help your prospects understand "what's in it for them" is to use or say the word *you*.

For example, *Don't* say, "The new system will use 50 percent less energy than the current system."

Do say: "*You* will save 50 percent on your energy bill with the new system."

To move away from the perspective of the seller and see yourself as the prospect, ask yourself these questions:

- Why should I, as a prospect, care about a specific feature of your product?
- How will I, as a prospect, really benefit from that feature?
- How does this feature contribute to reducing or eliminating my pain?

All too often when we are in the vendor's seat our thoughts are so centered around our selling objectives—our old brain only thinks about us—that we forget that our message is intended for our customers. By "wording with 'you,'" any of your Message Building Blocks can become customer-centric.

Look again at Figure 10-1, which was used to illustrate the use of claims. Count how many times Nationwide used the word *you* or *your* on that single page . . . The answer is 27 times.

Remember that rhetorical questions start with "What if you . . ." and you should close by asking, "What do *you* think?"

When you utilize the word *you*, your prospect's old brain will unconsciously experience owning and using your system. Your messages instantly becomes more personal, and the prospect will feel you are genuinely interested in helping them solve their pain.

> Messages instantly become old-brain friendly when using :you."

Most of us have been trained to sell the benefits instead of the features, but there is an even better way to communicate a point by using the word *you* in the process. Focusing on "you" beats focusing on benefits anyway—hands down, every time.

For example, suppose your task was to sell a copy machine. Look at three approaches you could take:

- *Poor:* "This copier comes with a sorter and a stapler." These are features.

- *Better:* "This copier will save you time by offering a sorter and stapler." This is a benefit followed by the features.

- *Best:* "Don't waste your time sorting or stapling!" This gives a cure to one of their areas of pain. If your prospect is pressed for time, this message goes to the old brain faster than the others. It hits with a concrete, personal message that suggests strong personal and financial gain.

WHAT TO REMEMBER

The Seven Impact Boosters add meaning and flair to the Six Message Building Blocks. As for the first, don't you listen better when someone talks *to* you instead of *at* you? Be sure that you deliver your message by wording with "you" . . . and we managed to say it three times in one sentence!

IMPACT BOOSTER #2: YOUR CREDIBILITY

Technique and technology are important.
But adding trust is the issue of the decade.
~TOM PETERS, AUTHOR & BUSINESS GURU

Your credibility factor will contribute a significant amount to your selling effectiveness. Although it is a subjective and difficult value to measure, you always know credibility when you see it. In *You've Got to Be Believed to Be Heard*, Bert Decker, founder and president of San Francisco-based Decker Communications, maintains that credibility is probably the most important factor to maximize your impact. In essence, your credibility is the core of what makes other people believe you. The old brain is very sensitive to credibility because it detects confidence or lack thereof.

Ultimately, credibility is a function of six qualities:

1. Your Creativity
2. Your Fearlessness
3. Your Passion
4. Your Integrity
5. Your Similarity
6. Your Expressiveness

Let's explore each of these variables.

CREDIBILITY VARIABLE #1: YOUR CREATIVITY

You won't be interesting unless you say things imaginatively, originally, freshly, creatively.
~WILLIAM BERNBACH, ADVERTISING EXPERT

When is the last time you felt you really used creativity to help other people understand you and differentiate you from your competition? How many times have you included a picture in the core of an e-mail to break the monotony and help your reader understand your message visually?

Recently, our company, SalesBrain, helped a major high-tech company win a multimillion-dollar deal by applying the most daring business creativity.

A large client of SalesBrain was bidding to be chosen as one of only three suppliers (from a field of eleven) in a highly visible international competition. The battle was fierce among all contenders.

Since thousands of pages of data containing product specifications and pricing tables for all bidders had already been delivered to the purchasing committee, we knew we needed a creative way to reach the old brain of the decision-makers, so that our client's claims would be remembered.

> Measure your "credibility factor" in order to increase your selling effectiveness.

Here's what happened. Ten days before the decision deadline, we purchased a Web domain name similar to the purchasing company's trade name and created an e-mail address for its CEO. This way, e-mails coming from him at that domain name would be perceived to be authentic.

Then, we generated an e-mail to all members of the purchasing committee that seemed to come from their CEO. The e-mail was dated sixteen months in the future and congratulated each member of the buying committee for achieving tremendous success as a result of choosing the right vendor—SalesBrain's client—sixteen months earlier.

The e-mail directed recipients to a Web site where they could view a complete multimedia presentation about our client. This presentation highlighted the benefits achieved by the use of our client's system during the sixteen months since the contract had supposedly been signed.

This was a very bold move. But less than four hours after we blasted the e-mail, every one of the twenty-six-member buying committee had opened the e-mail and visited the site! The impact was phenomenal.

Though some members were amazed by the fearlessness of our client, the message we sent was impossible to miss: our client was bold, creative, and committed to winning the business. Three months later, SalesBrain's client made the final cut as one of only three suppliers who landed the largest European contract in their industry.

The power of creativity is peerless, but being creative takes a lot of work. Most of us recognize the benefits of creativity, yet we typically stick with established routine because we know it takes time and effort to be truly creative.

Luckily, there is a shortcut to creativity—it's called variety. By using variety, you will help the old brain stay alert so your audience can be more open to your message.

Tips to Achieve Variety

1. *Include pictures, audio, or video segments whenever possible.* These types of additions stimulate the old brain.

2. *Vary colors in text or copy.* Colors affect your old brain at a subconscious level (Figure 15-1) according to Margaret Walch, director of the Color Association of the United States.

3. *Use a different medium than the status quo.* For example, if all the other presenters are using software like PowerPoint, use a flip chart or tell a story or enact a mini-drama. Observe the impact of just being different from all the "me-too" competitors.

4. *Use a different speed. Change the tone of your voice.* You can be unique just by telling your message differently.

Remember that all the effort you invest in being creative will translate into increased interest and attractiveness. This, in turn, translates immediately into an increased impact on the old brain.

Colors		
Color	**Symbolizes**	**Used By**
Red	Power, Activity, Rescue	Coca-Cola, Red Cross, Business 2.0
Pink	Calm, Feminism	Barbie, Pepto-Bismol, Mary Kay
Orange	Movement, Construction, Energy	Cingular Wireless, SalesBrain, Home Depot
Yellow	Light, Future, Philosophy	Kodak, National Geographic, Best Buy
Green	Money, Growth, Environment	John Deere, Starbucks, British Petroleum
Blue	Trust, Authority, Security	IBM, Microsoft, American Express
Purple	Royalty, Spirituality, New Age	Sun, Yahoo, Barney

FIGURE 15-1

CREDIBILITY VARIABLE #2:
YOUR FEARLESSNESS

Have you ever noticed how small dogs often bark at big dogs, but they rarely actually try to attack them? Why is that? Because the small dog's old brain detects the absence of fear from the big dog, so bark as it might, a small dog will never purposely put itself in danger and actually take action to attack the bigger dog. Similarly, your prospects should not detect any trace of your fear—of losing their business!

Fact: Most decisions are based on fear. The old brain is the specialized organ for processing fear, a fact echoed by Rush Dozier in *Fear Itself.* "The primitive fear system (located in the old brain) appears to be particularly attuned to detecting fear," states Dozier.

Imagine you are the purchasing manager of a large corporation. Your decision to sign a multimillion-dollar deal will be based on your fear. You could fear losing your job or missing your quarterly bonus. It is that very fear that will drive your decision.

> Be fearless and maintain low attachment to the outcome.

Remember the old days when IBM mainframes were dominant? There was a saying "No one ever gets fired for buying IBM." IBM cultivated that image of safety, which alleviated the fear their prospects had of unreliability.

The old brain can detect signs of fear that are invisible to the eye. Did you know that customs officers are trained to read signs of fear in people who may be hiding illegal goods? It has been proven, for example, that the smell of sweat signals to the old brain that a person is lying.

Also, according to LeDoux, "Our brains can detect danger before we even experience the feeling of being afraid. The brain also begins to initiate physical responses (heart palpitations, sweaty palms, muscle tension) before we become aware of an associated feeling of fear."

So how do we as sellers guard against showing signs of fear?

The opposite of fear is fearlessness. Fearlessness might also be called non-attachment. By displaying an attitude of high intention but low attachment to the outcome, you send a strong message to your prospect's decision-maker—the old brain—that you are motivated to win their business but that you have no fear of losing it.

Improving your Fearlessness

- *Act with high intention but low attachment.* Do your best, and then don't worry about the immediate outcome. Although your old brain might try to tell you otherwise, it is only business you are conducting. It is not a life-threatening event.
- *Keep a positive outlook.* Recent research such as the study published in *Emotional Contagion* by Professor Elaine Hatfield has demonstrated that emotions are contagious. Optimism doesn't cost you anything, and your prospect will most likely prefer to buy from somebody who is nice and positive . . . and perhaps your prospects will "catch" your positive attitude, thanking you in the process.
- *Remember that even the best and most brilliant people do not win 100 percent of the time.* Even so, those who are actively working on increasing their selling skills learn to harness their fears and transform the energy of the fear into something positive.
- *Practice, practice, practice.* If delivering your message includes public speaking, you will certainly experience some fear. In fact, in an extensive survey conducted by the *London Sunday Times*, statistics showed that most people are more afraid of speaking in public than they are of dying! (Readers ranked their fears in order: fear of public speaking was number one;

followed by fear of heights; fear of insects, bugs, and reptiles; fear of financial difficulties; fear of deep water; fear of sickness; and fear of death.)

So, you are not alone, and by practicing and rehearsing, you will not only improve the quality of your delivery to a public audience, but you will also slowly let go of your fear.

CREDIBILITY VARIABLE #3: YOUR PASSION

*Nothing great in the world has ever
been accomplished without passion.*
~G. HEGEL, GERMAN PHILOSOPHER

Question: Besides fame, what do the following people have in common?

- Pablo Picasso
- Albert Einstein
- Michael Jordan
- Martin Luther King, Jr.
- Mother Teresa

Answer: They were all passionate about what they did.

Have you ever heard Einstein talk about physics or Martin Luther King, Jr. speak about human rights? These celebrities' passion for their work brought them to an unequaled level of excellence. Their passion could be sensed by anyone who came in contact with them.

In his book, *Leading Out Loud*, Terry Pearce writes:

I have often asked customers and friends to identify the most effective leaders they know and to look at the source of their power as communicators of messages. Invariably, names such as J. F. Kennedy, Martin Luther King, Jr., Barbara Jordan, Winston Churchill, Mario Cuomo, and Ronald Reagan are mentioned. Certainly, these people had a command of their language, but as people point out, what stimulated others was neither the rhetoric nor the show; it was the conviction of the speaker, the energy, the passion for his or her cause, the extent to which that passion and that conviction were conveyed.

Passion is that intangible factor that you can sense without really knowing where it comes from. It is difficult, if not impossible, to fake, and, as with fear, your prospect's old brain can sense your passion as accurately as a speedometer measures your speed. Since emotions are contagious, if you are passionate, other people will become more enthusiastic as well. Psychology professor and scientist Elaine Hatfield testifies to this truth in her book *Emotional Contagion*, ". . . how could we have missed the pervasiveness of primitive emotional contagion?" Your passion can be detected in your words, your voice, and your body, and the best way to increase your passion is to be passionate about it!

How to Maximize Your Passion

- *Learn to measure your level of passion.* There may be a time of day when you are at your peak. For example, you may want to avoid making an important phone call with a prospect on a Monday morning if you had a major upset over the weekend. Your voice will not sound as self-confident as it normally would. Your best bet is to wait until later in the day when you have reestablished your natural level of passion.

- *Surround yourself with passionate people* because passion builds on itself.
- *Practice and rehearse.* Although practicing and rehearsing will not impact your passion, it will increase your professionalism and decrease your nervousness—both of which will help other people to see you as a passionate person.
- *Remember: you can never be too passionate*, and passion is contagious. If you are really enthusiastic about your product, your prospects will be too.
- *Do what you love, and love what you do.* It will be easy for your audience to sense your passion.

Remember the last time you met somebody passionate about something? Didn't you feel that person was interesting even if at first his or her field of passion wasn't high on your priority list? To increase your credibility, increase your passion.

CREDIBILITY VARIABLE #4: YOUR INTEGRITY

To give real service you must add something which cannot be bought or measured with money. That is sincerity and integrity.
~DOUGLAS ADAMS, ENGLISH NOVELIST

How many customer relationships, how many personal relationships, have ended because one or more of the players did not tell the truth, the whole truth, and nothing but the truth?

Are you in your business for the long run? Do you care if you sell your prospect something he or she will not really benefit from? Will you be present when problems arise after the sale? Did you perform an honest diagnosis of your prospect's pain, or did you hide a few things under the rug?

Meeting your commitments, making decisions that are based on what is good for your prospects, and walking your talk may all have an immediate cost for you, but they will serve you well in the long run. A number of large companies are devising careful mission statements just to define what it means to act with integrity.

How to Show Integrity

- *Don't fake it*. Just be you. It's much better to be you and focus on your strengths than to pretend you are somebody else. Maybe you are a little shy and don't exude passion, or perhaps you are not a very aggressive salesperson. That's perfectly acceptable. Inconsistency, inappropriate body language, or misrepresentation can cause your prospect's old brain to go on the alert. The brain interprets inconsistency as possible danger.
- *Be honest*. Saying, "Sure, my system can do this or that" may be a shortcut to getting an order, but lies (even "half-ones") often lead to self-destruction.
- *Know when to say "no" or "I don't know."* There will be times when admitting limitations or lack of knowledge will gain greater respect from your prospects.

Much of the communication with the old brain happens at the subconscious level. When you communicate with integrity, you have no fear of being trapped in deception. The sensitive fear sensors in the old brain of your audience are not triggered: they sense a perfect alignment between you and what you say. The ultimate result is that your audience will trust you more.

CREDIBILITY VARIABLE #5: YOUR SIMILARITY

*If you wish to persuade me, you must think my
thoughts, feel my feelings, and speak my words.*
~CICERO, ROMAN ORATOR & STATESMAN

Let's face it, we all like people who are similar to us. Your old brain is simply more open to people who look, sound, and act like you do because it is able to relax its guard against the unknown or unpredictable. In fact, in *Fear Itself*, Rush Dozier points out that the anxiety we feel regarding strangers could be an important element in the widespread fear of public speaking, since we tend not to be afraid to speak around our closest friends and family—even a large group of them.

The trained salesperson knows that for a healthy, relaxed atmosphere, he needs to identify with his audience and show them he relates to them. Indeed, a huge amount of research known as Neuro Linguistic Programming (NLP) demonstrates that highlighting similarities between yourself and your prospect makes your solution much more appealing.

NLP can be defined as the science of using the language of the mind to create more effective communication. It is an innovative approach enabling people to organize information and perceptions in ways that allow results once thought inconceivable. NLP is about modeling human excellence through specific techniques that allow an insight into the detailed mechanics of how people structure activities.

NLP is one of hundreds of studies showing that we like people who are similar to us and are familiar. Here's an example of similarity in action.

A few years ago, I was working for John Metcalfe, an executive at Silicon Graphics. John was a seasoned salesperson who came with many years of experience in the field. He wore expensive dark

> To be trusted, look, feel, and sound like your prospect's best friend.

Italian suits and had a soft but persuasive voice. A Scot by origin, after many years of experience in corporate America, John had learned to wear a white shirt and a red tie with elegance.

That morning, the two of us were hosting the dean of the University of Bombay, India—the largest university in the world. His college boasted a gigantic pool of exceedingly smart students and a decent budget for new computers. This was an important meeting indeed.

John and I had agreed to meet fifteen minutes early to discuss the objectives of the meeting and to review the agenda. When John walked in the door, I was shocked to see him wearing a brown suit and a striped blue tie. I have never been focused on fashion, but I suppressed the urge to make a wisecrack about how unstylish and unattractive the color of his suit was. As John happened to be my boss, I refrained from commenting.

Minutes later, the dean from the University of Bombay walked in. To my big surprise, he was wearing almost the exact same suit and tie as John! John introduced me to him; he had met the dean in Bombay previously, and it was obvious the two men had a strong rapport. The meeting went extremely well.

As it happened, when John and I debriefed after the meeting, John brought up the subject of his suit himself.

"What do you think of my suit?" he grinned. John proceeded to tell me that he had met the dean twice in India, and each time the dean was wearing the same suit. So, John was inspired to dig in his garage to find a suit that our visitor could relate to.

A few months later, we closed a multimillion-dollar order with the University of Bombay. Obviously we did not win the deal just because John wore the same suit as the dean, but I know it didn't hurt! I myself witnessed that John was able to establish a very high level of trust with the dean . . . in just three short meetings.

Here's another interesting example. Recently my wife, Nathalie, received a postcard mailer for DSL services offered by California's Pacific Bell. The card was addressed specifically to her and showed a picture of a confident, attractive, smiling woman drinking a cup of coffee.

The very same day, I personally received a similar postcard from the same company, but the picture on the front was that of a man sitting in a trendy chair with a slogan that implied I might be boring if I work too much.

Each postcard advertised the exact same product, but targeted different genders. Knowing that typically men will relate to men, and women will relate to other women, Pacific Bell created customized covers and messages and sent them to respective genders.

Pacific Bell knew that by customizing the ads to their target markets, their prospects would better relate to the message and therefore be more open to suggestions. They evidently recognized that an increased impact on their prospects' old brain far outweighed the cost of designing and printing two different ads.

Do you take the time to customize your message to fit the profile of your prospects? Or do you copy and paste your PowerPoint slides from a template with the hope that "one message fits all"?

To be accessible to your prospects, align yourself with your target audience; tailor your message to address their specific pain. When your prospect's old brain perceives you as its "best friend" with little or no difference between the two of you, it relaxes and becomes more receptive to your message. It is easier to buy from people who look like you, sound like you, and talk as if they really know and understand you.

Similarity is good. Neuro Linguistic Programming studies have demonstrated that when two people communicate in a nonthreatening environment, they will adopt a common language, a common voice, and a common posture. They will even start to breathe in synchronicity. (And, yes, breathing is also controlled by the old brain; it's all subconscious.)

CREDIBILITY VARIABLE #6: YOUR EXPRESSIVENESS

If I went back to college again, I'd concentrate on two areas: learning to write and to speak before an audience. Nothing in life is more important than the ability to communicate effectively.

~GERALD FORD, THIRTY-EIGHTH US PRESIDENT

Expressiveness. It's all in the words you choose, right? Wrong. Several prominent communications specialists, including Professor

Albert Mehrabian of UCLA, have demonstrated that 7 percent of the impact of your communication comes from your words—the verbal component of your message—while 38 percent comes from your voice—the vocal aspect of your message—and 55 percent is achieved with your body language—the visual component of your message (Figure 15-2).

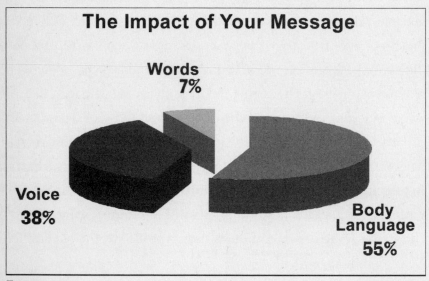

FIGURE 15-2

In *Delivering Dynamic Presentations: Using Your Voice and Body for Impact,* Ralph Hillmann, PhD, professor of speech communications, also demonstrates how your voice and body posture can make all the difference in how well your message is understood: from effective pitch patterns to the amazing impact of posture.

In other words, it's not what you say; it's how you say it. When you deliver your message in person, how well you express yourself depends on three factors:

1. Your Words
2. Your Voice
3. Your Body Language

Expressiveness: Your Words

> *The difference between "almost the right word"*
> *and the "right word" is the difference between*
> *a lightning bug and lightning.*
>
> ~MARK TWAIN, AMERICAN AUTHOR

When you simply want to inform an audience, the written medium is best. Facts and information are efficiently transferred to others in writing, since, statistically, you read about five times faster than you speak. However, writing typically activates only rational thinking, handled by the new brain instead of the true decision-maker, the old brain.

When you want to persuade—to move people to make decisions and to take action—speak to them. Spoken information, especially when you are face-to-face, carries your energy and passion and generates more emotion than written words do. It impacts the old brain much more powerfully.

When it comes to your words, two rules apply:

- Your words must be *carefully chosen*. Finding the exact words will help maximize the impact of your delivery.
- It is vital that you *minimize the number of written words you use*, especially when displayed on slides.

While you are choosing which words to use, be sure to avoid words, habits, or speech patterns that decrease your credibility.

DON'Ts of Communication
For effective communication, DON'T:

- *Use words that your audience may not understand,* such as undefined acronyms or jargon that will not commonly be recognized by your listeners.
- *Use expressions like "I think," "I believe," or "hopefully."* These types of phrases dilute your message and your conviction. (They are also redundant.)
- *Use non-words like "uh," "umm," or habitual "like"s or "ya know"s.* These distract your listeners.
- *Use complex sentences.* During World War II, US Defense authorities printed posters that read, "Illumination must be extinguished when premises are vacated." When seeing one of these for the first time, President Roosevelt exclaimed, "Why can't they just say, 'Put out the lights when you leave'?"
- *Use words that are too abstract or that do not give a precise measure of a benefit.* For example, avoid saying, "We are a leading provider of . . ." or "We provide a flexible, integrated, scalable solution to . . . ." These phrases are not tangible enough for the old brain to get a solid visual picture of the meaning.
- *Repeat what's already written on your slide, or worse, read your slides word for word.* Your audience can read faster than you can talk. Your slides should support your message, but they are not your message.

- *Say, "I will try to demonstrate . . ."* Either you will demonstrate it or you won't, but you should not try to.

Just as certain words and phrases hinder your credibility factor, other types of communication help it.

DOs of Communication
To increase your Credibility Factor, DO

- *Utilize pauses.* Short silences give your audience time to process your information. They also help highlight an important point.
- *Use simple, precise, and concrete words.* Vague claims and generalizations don't connect, and thesaurus words don't impress.
- *Use the specialized vocabulary of your prospects.* Remember, the old brain will open up to someone who's "one of us," so use the same language/lingo of your prospects.
- *Use short and simple sentences.* Point made.

You are not alone in seeking to find the best, most concise language to use in your presentations. In fact, several studies have done some of the legwork for you. David Peoples, in his book *Presentations Plus*, references a study done at Yale University that lists the twelve most persuasive words in the English language as these:

1. You
2. Money
3. Save

7. Health
8. Safety
9. Love

4. New
5. Results
6. Easy

10. Discovery
11. Proven
12. Guarantee

Furthermore, David Peoples also lists the most powerful combinations of words as:

1. Thank you.
2. Would you please?
3. What do you think?
4. I am proud of you.

So you see, you don't have to earn a PhD in linguistics or a masters in communication to be an effective speaker! Just start by using *you* a lot, and be positive and polite!

Expressiveness: Your Voice

> *Surely whoever speaks to me in the right voice,*
> *him or her I shall follow.*
>
> ~WALT WHITMAN, NINETEENTH-CENTURY AMERICAN POET

Is your voice as good as it can be as a selling tool? A study done at UCLA found that when speaking on the phone, 84 percent of your message is conveyed by the music of your voice, a combination of your pitch, tone, tempo, and rhythm. Furthermore, brain researchers have discovered that the old brain has highly sensitive credibility detectors. These detectors are pre-verbal, meaning they are activated by tone of voice and body language, not by words. How often do you actively work on improving your voice to have more impact on your prospect's old brain?

The human voice is characterized by six parameters:

1. Pitch
2. Tone
3. Tempo
4. Rhythm
5. Emphasis
6. Pauses

To find the most effective voice to reach your audience's old brain, first think about what is the worst. Instinctively, we know that people who are loud and/or who speak aggressively are not listener-friendly. Our old brain feels threatened, rushed, or confronted with noise in such settings.

The most effective voice to reach the old brain is your "best friend" voice. When you use your best friend voice, you address your audience on an equal level, and it maximizes your accessibility factor: you avoid sounding like the stereotypical salesperson.

In *The Cluetrain Manifesto*, ranked one of *Business Week*'s Top Ten Books of 2000, authors Levine, Locke, Searles, and Weinberger develop a powerful theory that the Web is creating a gap between humans and corporations because of the difference of voice, as explained in this extract:

Whether explaining or complaining, joking or serious, the human voice is unmistakably genuine. It can't be faked. Most corporations, on the other hand, only know how to talk in the soothing, humorless monotone of the mission statement, marketing brochure, and your-call-is-important-to-us busy signal. Same old tone, same old lies. No wonder networked markets have no respect for companies unable or unwilling to speak as they do. But learning to speak in a human voice is not some trick, nor will corporations convince us they are human with lip service about "listening to customers." They will only sound human when they empower real human beings to speak on their behalf.

When you speak to your friends, you naturally vary your voice: your tone is deep and you pause frequently to think, emote, or emphasize a point. Pausing adds clarity and emphasis. Varying your voice reflects good energy and projects feeling.

Finding Your Voice

What concrete actions can you take to improve your voice? First of all, research has proven that a voice with a lower pitch is more persuasive. So if you have some control of your voice, lower your pitch; and if you don't, you can learn how to lower your pitch like a professional actor. Voice coaches will accept clients other than actors; they also help politicians and businesspeople.

What is the ideal tempo or speed—slow, average, or fast? Again, research shows that people who speak about 20 percent faster than average have more influence. Speaking fast typically demonstrates passion, and your audience's old brain will detect it.

In the workplace, if the message you will be delivering involves your voice, tape yourself and listen. Then practice your "best friend voice" in front of a mirror and pretend you are giving this presentation to your closest buddies!

If you really want to improve your speaking voice, ask your friends or colleagues what they think about it. Take the time to analyze it constructively; when is the last time you audio- or videotaped yourself during a presentation and carefully listened to your voice? Are you believable? Do you sound professorial, dry, or distant? Is your voice too high or airy? Do you say "uh," "um," or "ya know" a lot? Do you speak too quickly? Do you effectively vary your voice like you would normally do when you are talking to your best friends?

Remember, your words account for only 7 percent of your impact while your voice accounts for at least 38 percent. Instead of spending hours wordsmithing a presentation, you may want to spend that time fine-tuning your voice for a mini-drama. Focus on the areas with maximum impact on your audience's old brain. And whenever you present, whether it's to one person or ten thousand, speak to your audience as if they were your best friends.

Expressiveness: Your Body Language

> Stand tall. The difference between towering and cowering
> is totally a matter of inner posture. It's got nothing
> to do with height, it costs nothing, and it's more fun.
> ~MALCOLM FORBES, AMERICAN PUBLISHER

How is it possible that some people are so much more believable than others, even when they say the same words with the same voice?

The old brain can quickly read your body language. Without even bringing this information to the conscious level, it will immediately disqualify or emphasize what you are trying to communicate.

A huge amount of research exists on the topic of body language.

Sifting through it, one can find the most important body language management strategies for salespeople. To maximize your positive effect on the old brain, incorporate the following habits into your presentations:

Maintain strong posture and purposeful movement. For example, imagine your hands drawing a large circle in front of you as you say, "You will be able to gather a vast amount of scientific data." Putting the emphasis on the word *vast* at the same time as your hand moves really conveys a stronger meaning to the word.

Use gestures and facial expressions to reflect energy and attitude. We all respond better to animated speakers than to lifeless ones. As you seek to connect with the audience, keep in mind that of all the body clues you send to your audience, eye contact is the most important one.

Make sure you always remain facing your audience. Turning your back to the audience, even for a moment, greatly diminishes your credibility factor. The old brain will not hear what you are saying if it doesn't feel that it is being addressed personally. People often turn when reading PowerPoint slides from a screen, or when writing on a flip chart or whiteboard: prepare your visuals in advance or stand to the side of the board if you must.

Dress appropriately and be aligned with your listeners. Most of us would never appear in jeans and a t-shirt at a formal wedding. In the same way, avoid looking radically different from your prospects. The key word is similarity, or what NLP experts commonly call "mirroring."

Use as much space as reasonably possible. A common mistake people make when speaking in public is staying motionless behind a counter.

It sends a signal that you are afraid of moving in front of the audience. When you take control of the stage (and your audience's attention), your fearlessness greatly increases your credibility factor.

Involve the audience. This includes asking the audience to move, say key points, or answer questions that may otherwise have been rhetorical.

Just as it is important to work on your voice, you will notice that practicing your body language is time well spent. Do not hesitate to videotape yourself and review your body language.

Check the following:

- *Is your body totally still, or are you moving too much?* Too much movement, especially if the movements are not purposeful, or too much rigidity may send a signal that you lack confidence. Remember, you should sound and look like the best friend of your audience.
- *Are you making any movements that are distracting for the audience?* You may be unconsciously touching your hair, tapping your pen, or jingling the change in your pockets.
- *Are you varying your voice and your body attitudes* to reflect your energy, your trustworthiness, and your message? (And to keep the old brain of your audience awake!)
- *Are your movements synchronized with your words?* You may want to practice the following exercise for a friend or in front of a mirror:
  1. Say the following sentence without any facial expression or movement, and with a monotone voice: "You will be able to gather a vast amount of scientific data that . . ."

2. Repeat the same phrase, putting emphasis on the words *you* and *vast*.

3. Repeat the sentence again, but add a gesture by describing a large circle with both arms precisely when you pronounce the word *vast*.

4. Notice what happens if you say the same sentence and trigger your arm movement when you say the word *data*.

5. Notice what happens if instead of drawing a large circle with your arms, you bring your hands close to each other, a gesture typically associated with something small.

Expressiveness: Your Eye Contact

As mentioned above, although your audience will react to many aspects of your body language, the most important is eye contact. Communication experts even call it "eye communication."

> To build trust, make eye contact for at least four seconds.

When your eyes meet the eyes of your audience, your old brain makes a direct connection. If your audience is made up of several people, it is important that you make eye contact with every one of them for at least four to five seconds. This will seem like a very long time, but people naturally do this when they converse with their best friends. When you are not making eye contact, the message you are sending is that you are not trustworthy. Regardless of what you say to your audience of decision-makers, their old brain will not hear it.

Improper eye communication includes staring at the back wall, staring at your feet or at the floor in front of you, making eye contact with only one or two people, breaking the eye contact in the middle of the sentence or in the middle of a thought, and making eye contact for two seconds or less. Lack of appropriate, extended eye communication reduces your ability to conduct a "best friend discussion" with each person in the audience.

Here is a dramatic example of the value of eye communication adapted from *Integrity Selling* by Ron Willingham.

How Eye Contact Saved His Life

In the midst of the Vietnam War, a young American soldier named Robert and his platoon were pinned down in a bunker by enemy fire. Robert's fellow soldiers were all killed, and he himself was hit three times—in his right shoulder, his right thigh, and his left side.

Lying on the ground weak and bloody, Robert realized that, at any moment, he was going to die. He visualized his heart pumping all the blood out of his left side . . . and then stopping completely . . . and then he'd be dead.

At that moment, some Vietcong soldiers arrived and started going through the dead American soldiers' bodies and taking their valuables—watches, rings, money, even knocking gold fillings out of their teeth.

Robert watched in panic as one of the soldiers made his way over to Robert, reached down for his watch, and discovered he was still alive. Immediately, the enemy soldier pointed his gun between Robert's eyes. This time, there was no doubt in his mind: Robert knew he was about to die.

In panic and despair, he looked up into the Vietcong soldier's eyes, and, with as much feeling and emotion as he could muster, shook his head vehemently from side to side and said: "No . . . no . . . please don't kill me!"

After several tense moments, the enemy soldier could no longer bear the emotional burden. Breaking eye contact, he put the gun to his side. Just then, another Vietcong soldier yelled something, and the soldier responded.

Robert understood intuitively that the other soldier had asked if he was still alive and that the first soldier had answered in the affirmative. Then the other soldier yelled again. Robert assumed he yelled, "Kill him!" because once again the soldier pointed his gun at him and was about to pull the trigger.

Again, Robert looked deeply into the enemy's eyes, shook his head from side to side, and said, "No . . . no . . . please don't kill me, please don't!"

After an incredibly painful pause, even though he couldn't understand the language, the Vietcong soldier once again backed down, broke eye contact, and dropped his gun to his side. Then he did something amazing: he pointed the gun into the ground a few feet away from where Robert lay and pulled the trigger. He didn't look at Robert again. He yelled something to the other soldier, and walked away.

After that amazing story, a disclaimer: All the concepts presented in this book apply to and have been tested on audiences from countries as different from each other as Argentina, Australia, Belgium, Brazil, China, France, Germany, India, Indonesia, Italy, Japan, South Korea, the United Kingdom, Spain, the United States, and many more.

After all, old brain behavior is typically completely independent from our cultural backgrounds. In *How Customers Think*, Zaltman writes,

"Consumers from very different cultures share a great deal, and their commonalities outnumber their differences." That's because the old brain comes from the evolutionary process of mankind and therefore follows the same practical laws regardless of our cultural or ethnic origins.

However, the one exception to techniques used in Selling to the Old Brain relates to eye communication. In some Asian cultures, too much eye contact can be perceived as aggressive and disrespectful. Therefore, it is highly recommended that you inquire about local practices in specific cultures before applying the four-second, direct eye-to-eye communication with your audience.

All of these habits of expression we've discussed need to become second nature to you in order to reinforce your impact. *Practice is absolutely critical.* Practice until you don't even need to think about it. For example, your ability to establish eye contact for four or five seconds should become completely automatic, so that all of your energy can be used to deliver your message passionately.

In summarizing how to best express yourself, remember the following: Your words may account for only 7 percent of your impact, but choose them carefully. Word with *you*. Mirror your audience, including body posture, dress, appearance, voice, and language. A practiced, polished voice and body language, combined with synchronized, purposeful movement and proper eye communication, are strategic influencing tools for expressing yourself both powerfully and authentically.

WHAT TO REMEMBER

Credibility is an important, intangible quality that largely depends on six different variables:

1. Your Creativity: Dare to be different.
2. Your Fearlessness: Demonstrate self-confidence.
3. Your Passion: Enthusiasm is contagious.
4. Your Integrity: It is the only way to go.
5. Your Similarity: Identify with your audience.
6. Your Expressiveness: Reinforce your message with your words, voice, and body language.

IMPACT BOOSTER #3: CONTRAST

There is no quality in this world that is not what it is merely by contrast. Nothing exists in itself.
~HERMAN MELVILLE, AUTHOR

You've likely heard the story about what happens when you drop a frog in a pot of water. If so, you know that the frog's reaction depends on one thing: the temperature of that water. If you drop him in hot water, the sharp contrast in temperatures triggers the frog's old brain to want to jump out fast. Yet put the same frog in lukewarm water and slowly turn up the heat, and the frog may sit there until he dies. Without the temperature contrast, there's no reason to jump.

That is exactly how our old brain works: a sharp contrast is often needed to help it make a decision. So in a sales context, the absence of contrast—especially when a prospect has difficulty understanding the differences between your product and others—will bring the prospect's decision-making ability to a halt.

> Sharp contrast helps your prospect's old brain make a decision more quickly and easily.

Consider this question: What outdoor temperature do you consider *hot*? If you have ever been in downtown London when the temperature climbs above 75 degrees F, you will see hordes of businessmen out in the street without their shirts on! Yet the same temperature would be considered pleasant, even mild, for people living in Florida. It's all relative—and it's all about contrast.

How much contrast do you have in your messages?

CREATING CONTRAST

Trying to create contrast by simply using text documents or PowerPoint presentations is very difficult. However, mini-dramas, contrasted big pictures, and stories can easily generate contrast.

Contrast often requires creativity. For example, you could first show your prospect how life without your product is painful, complex, or expensive. Then you could contrast that pain with the new painless, easy, or inexpensive life they would have if they used your solution.

A few years ago I was invited as a keynote speaker for a Linux conference in Korea. The room held over 2,200 people, and the speaker before me had made a rather generic presentation. I noticed in the dim light of the room that the audience was starting to fall asleep.

After a short introduction by the master of ceremonies, I calmly asked to have "the next slide please" of the total of four I was planning to use that day.

People were starting to resettle back into their sleepy poses when the fun began! Using a fake phone, I pretended my presentation was interrupted by a phone call from our IT (Information Technology) director who had yet another problem with a major software vendor. Obviously I was not happy, and while still on my call, I got into a serious argument with our IT director. I complained that the bug they had run into had been discovered three months earlier and that the vendor had promised to fix it, but nothing had happened. Now we had over four hundred users who were unable to access their emails for more than twenty-four hours.

At this point, I covered the phone with my hand and apologized to the crowd, who was still amazed that I had apparently interrupted my speech in front of thousands of people for a call about our IT system. When I "ended" the call, I told my audience I knew they could relate because they had probably all had a similar experience at one time or another.

Then, changing my tone of voice to a more relaxed and deeper tone—to emphasize the contrast—I said, "Let's imagine what your life would have been like if you had been using Linux. How would the phone call have been different? The answer is: you wouldn't get an embarrassing phone call in front of a large audience. Why? Because your IT director would have reported the problem by posting a bug report on the Web and, within a couple of hours, a Linux developer in the community would have had already e-mailed him a patch."

I felt the whole audience relax as the room erupted in a wave of whispers and dinner-table discussions.

Later that day, over two hundred people from the audience came to tell me how much they had enjoyed my little plot. The contrast between the first situation and the second one had helped them understand the message at an old brain level.

When seeking to use contrast to your advantage, think of it in terms of

- Before/After
- Without Your Solution/With Your Solution
- You/Your Competitors
- Now/Later

Remember that the old brain is truly wired to pay attention to contrast. In fact, recent research on our senses suggests that we are not just passively noticing changes such as change of sounds, lighting, and such; we are actually proactively scanning the environment to detect changes. This means that serving up contrast to the old brain of your audience is serving what is already "watched for" unconsciously. Think of contrast as a shortcut to attention and a fuel to processing.

Contrast can be used in different ways. You can show how your solution will move your prospect from a negative situation to a better situation. Or it can be used to emphasize something painful about a situation, especially if you want to undermine your competitors.

Every one of us who has lived in the age of media saturation has been influenced by contrast in advertising. We have all seen the typical example of an ad with two images featuring a bald person on the left, the "before" picture, and the same person with a full head of hair on the right side, the "after" picture. As discussed in chapter 9, the contrasted big picture is one way to showcase our second Message Building Block in selling. Without having to use complicated theories or fancy applications, contrast cuts to the "heart" of the old brain's thought. When we see a typical ad with two images—a shriveled up patch of weeds on the left (before), and a yard bursting in blooms on the right (after)—we immediately understand the proof of gain for the advertised product.

Contrast works because the old brain "gets it" without effort.

Let's close this chapter with another example of contrast in action. How hard did your brain have to work to comprehend the message?

FIGURE 16-1

WHAT TO REMEMBER

The old brain often needs sharp contrast to nudge it into making a decision. Without contrast, decision-making is often stalled. With a little creativity, you can help your prospects "get" the pain, claim, and gain, all through a little negative-to-positive contrast.

IMPACT BOOSTER #4:
EMOTION

*You've got to say it in such a way that people will feel it
in their gut. Because if they don't feel it, nothing will happen.*
~WILLIAM BERNBACH, ADVERTISING GURU

Do you remember where you were on July 20, 1969, or on September 11, 2001? Likely you do, yet you may not remember what you ate for lunch yesterday. The emotions attached to a significant event are powerful memory-makers.

Many of us think that emotions are things that happen to us. In reality, according to Robert Cooper and Ayman Sawaf in their book

Executive EQ, emotions are an inner source of energy, information, and influence.

The very root of the word emotion is *motere*, from the Latin verb "to move," and the prefix *e*, which denotes "to move away." This origin suggests that a tendency to act or to decide is implicit in every emotion. Thousands of years after the Romans defined the word for emotion, neuroscientists have confirmed that only emotions can trigger decisions.

Since emotion is one of the six stimuli that reach the old brain, the fastest way to influence your audience is through the heart, not the head. Whenever we experience a strong emotion, our brain creates a cocktail of hormones that acts as a memory-maker and a decision trigger. Rush Dozier, in *Fear Itself*, quotes, "The stronger our feelings, the more vivid and long lasting our memories . . . this applies to learning as well."

Multiple studies on the brain have clearly demonstrated that strong emotions do accelerate and strengthen synaptic connections between our neurons. We have more than 100 billion neurons in the gray matter of our brains. Individually, they are unremarkable. But when they connect with one another, magic happens. A lot of that magic has to do with the way we remember.

Dale Carnegie, renowned author of *How to Win Friends and Influence People*, said in another of his books, *Public Speaking*, "When dealing with people, remember, you are not dealing with creatures of logic, but with creatures of emotion."

What are powerful memories for you? Driving a car for the very first time? Hearing about the birth or the death of someone dear to you? What you did the day of your graduation or the night of your wedding?

We are often surprised at how well we can recall vivid details of events that happened a long time ago. There is a scientifically documented reason that our brains make memories: it's called *emotional marking*.

THE SCIENCE OF FEELINGS

When we have strong emotional reactions to a person or event, the cocktail of hormones that is released into our bloodstream accelerates and intensifies the synaptic connections in our brain. If the emotion felt was very intense, like at a wedding, a birth, or a particularly affecting event, only one occurrence of the experience is enough to create a lifelong memory.

I recently came across a visual ad from a software company similar to the one shown here (Figure 17-1). This concept uses perspective as a grabber to create powerful emotion in the company's prospects.

> No emotion, no decision. Powerful emotions mark your old brain and reach straight to its core.

Because the picture is taken from the perspective of a person traveling at high speed across rocky terrain, and because your old brain is self-centered, your first tendency is to place yourself in the same position, causing you to feel as if you are also in a precarious position. This is a very good example of even a print ad's ability to create an emotional and personal experience for the old brain.

In the book *The Emotional Brain*, Joseph LeDoux explains how a baby in the womb experiences the same pounding heart and muscle tension his mother feels as she experiences fright if she slips and falls.

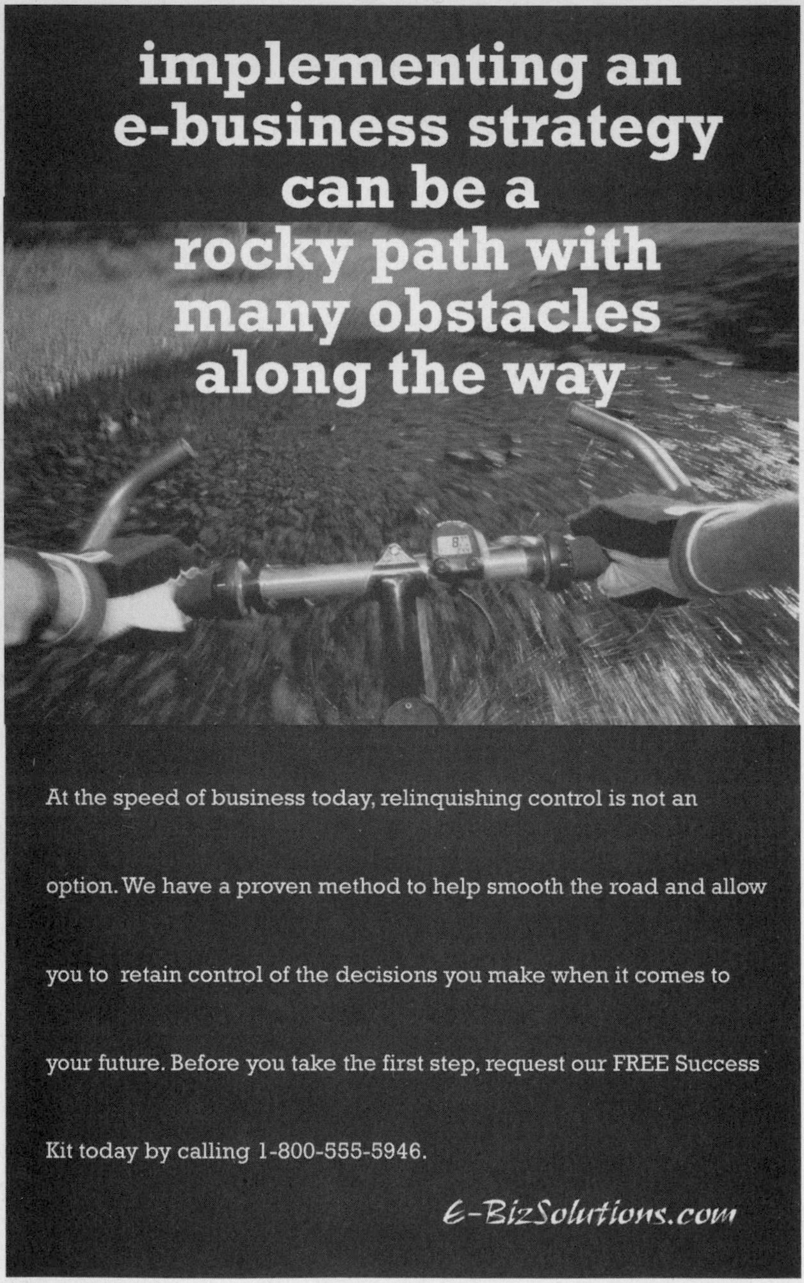

implementing an e-business strategy can be a rocky path with many obstacles along the way

At the speed of business today, relinquishing control is not an option. We have a proven method to help smooth the road and allow you to retain control of the decisions you make when it comes to your future. Before you take the first step, request our FREE Success Kit today by calling 1-800-555-5946.

E-BizSolutions.com

FIGURE 17-1

The baby associates the feelings with fear of falling and later relives the same symptoms as an adult when the plane he is flying on experiences turbulence. The hormones released by the mother have created a strong associative memory in the baby's brain.

EXPERIMENTING WITH EMOTIONS

Pretend for a moment that your advertising firm has been assigned to educate parents on the issue of kids using products like paints, glue solvents, or any other common home products as potentially lethal drugs. What approach would you take?

Now study the ad targeting parents whose kids may have access to spray cans inside their homes (Figure 17-2). What kind of emotion does this picture generate in you? How long does it take you to understand the issue?

Emotions involve what we often call a "gut feeling," instinct, or intuition. Although many of us have been trained to follow our heads, which are dominated by our logical left brains, research has proven that we should be more willing to follow our hearts. There is a dramatic and distinct connection between our right brain, emotion, and the impact it can have on the old brain.

In a revealing experiment, Professor Antonio Damasio proved that the subconscious part of our old brain becomes aware of critical facts before they actually reach our consciousness.

Damasio gave test subjects four decks of cards. They were asked to pick a card from any of the four decks, and then turn it over. Two decks were rigged to produce an overall loss—in play money—and two to produce a gain.

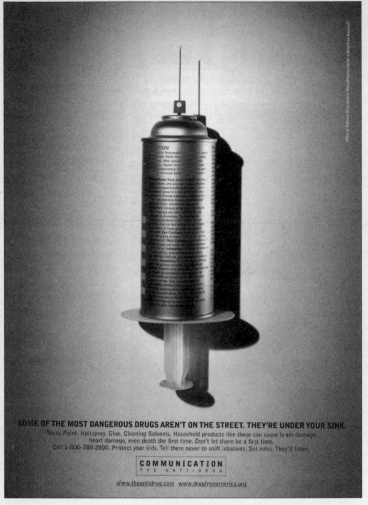

FIGURE 17-2   PARTNERSHIP FOR A DRUG-FREE AMERICA

At intervals, the participants were asked what they thought was going on in the game. Meanwhile, they were hooked up to sensors similar to those used in lie-detector machines to measure skin conductance responses (SCRs).

By the time the test subjects turned over about ten cards, they began showing a measurable, physical reaction in the form of SCRs whenever they reached for a losing deck. But, not until they had turned, on average, thirty cards, could subjects verbalize their "hunch" that two of the decks were riskier. It took twenty more cards, or a total of fifty, before they could explain why their hunch was right.

Some players were never able to put their hunches into words, yet they, too, showed elevated SCRs and picked more often from the decks that provided more rewards. Even if they couldn't explain it, their old brain had detected the two decks that were favorable.

Do you remember the story of the presentation I gave in Korea at a Linux conference? After doing the mini-drama on the phone, I wanted to create more emotion in delivering the proof of gain. Just after the fake phone conversation, I pressed the next slide button on my laptop. Unfortunately, instead of having the next slide, my computer locked and displayed a full blue screen with a "fatal error detected" message—the operating system had crashed and now my laptop would most likely require several long minutes to reboot. At that point, I couldn't disguise my panic: I looked desperate.

The audience, many of whom were still processing the phone mini-drama, found it quite ironic that a Linux evangelist at a Linux conference was not running Linux on his own computer—a deadly sin in that environment. Then, against all reason, I proceeded to ask for the next slide! Now people in the audience started to feel that I was crazy: how could my laptop instantly display the next slide when it had just crashed?!

At that time U-Jin Kim, the CEO of LinuxOne who was the main sponsor for this event and who had invited me to present, was showing serious distress: he thought I had completely lost it. It was time to deliver the punch line: To everyone's surprise, the next slide appeared immediately, as I said, "Oh, I forgot! This couldn't happen because indeed I am running Linux on my laptop," and I showed them my desktop with the Linux interface. I had just demonstrated the value of a solid operating system using only a slide with a fake blue screen and an error message.

Just imagine the emotion that the people in the room experienced that day! I didn't simply deliver the message at a rational level. Both the phone mini-drama and the supposedly locked-up laptop had generated an emotional response in the audience. The result was unequivocal: I gathered over two hundred business cards of the top IT companies in Korea that day, and U-Jin called me repeatedly in the years to follow to offer me the job of CEO of his American subsidiary.

Now think about some of your past presentations or messages. Did you communicate at a purely rational level, or did you instill some emotions in your audience? If you were a prospect at one of your usual presentations, would you feel compelled to act, or even to remember the presentation beyond a few hours or days?

In this book, you have seen the value of emotion-stirring messages. You have read about salespeople who, through creativity and a little courage, spoke their message through a mini-drama that showed the life of a prospect before and after their solution, and thus were able to automatically evoke strong emotional responses. Creating an emotional message is not always easy, but if you follow the guidelines of Selling to the Old Brain, your presentations will naturally generate emotions and consequently create lasting memories of you and your message.

WHAT TO REMEMBER

Delivering your message only at the rational level is not enough to convince the old brain. You have to generate emotion to help your customer decide to buy from you. Mini-dramas are especially powerful emotion-inducers, but people will also respond emotionally to compelling stories, strong contrasts, and "you"-focused claims.

Any of your Message Building Blocks can have emotion . . . be creative!

18

IMPACT BOOSTER #5: LEARNING STYLES

A wise teacher makes learning a joy.
~Traditional English Proverb

Some people like to hear information. Some like to see the big picture before knowing the details. Some like to "sleep on" new information before making a move. Others need to feel an experience to better understand.

Peter Drucker, a preeminent business philosopher and prolific author, has pointed out that one of the most important things you can learn about yourself is your information-gathering style. In fact, people use three different channels to learn: *visual*, *auditory*, and *kinesthetic*. These channels gather and process information in different ways:

- The visual channel depends on *seeing* to learn.
- The auditory channel relies on *hearing* to learn.
- The kinesthetic channel uses *touch* to learn.

Do you know which style you typically use to gather information? Let's do a test: *How many windows are there in your house or apartment?*

Do you have the answer? What did you do to process the number you came up with? Chances are, you visualized your place and counted each of the windows. You had to enter a visual mode to retrieve the information: an auditory or kinesthetic mode simply wouldn't work.

Indeed, the visual mode is the native mode of the old brain.

TUNING INTO THE CHANNELS

To better understand the ways different people learn, let's look at how the different learning channels are used to interpret different types of information.

The Visual channel can be used to interpret

- pictures or graphics
- images and icons
- props
- the visual component of a video or a printed ad
- the visual component of a well-told story, mini-drama, or demo.

Impact Booster #5: Learning Styles

Example in speech: If you say, "I saw the sun rising on this new era," your listener is forced to go into his/her visual mode and "see" what you are describing. This is because you used the verb "saw."

The Auditory channel is used to interpret elements such as

- any written text
- any spoken words
- the audio section of a movie or the legend in a picture
- the auditory portion of a well-told story.

Example in speech: If you say, "I heard the bell," then the auditory channel of your audience is stimulated.

The Kinesthetic channel is used

- when people are asked to perform tasks or exercises that involve touching or experiencing objects
- with props
- in the kinesthetic portion of a good story or a mini-drama.

Example in speech: If you say, "The sun heated the asphalt until it was as hot as fire," it evokes the kinesthetic channel because heat can be experienced through touch.

All three channels are used in:

- well-told stories
- well-acted mini-dramas
- demos in which the audience is involved.

Although you use all three channels to learn, research shows that everyone has one channel that is more effective or more developed than the others. In fact, according to Genie Laborde, communication authority and author of *Influencing with Integrity*, statistically, 40 percent of people are primarily visual, 20 percent are strongly auditory, and 40 percent are kinesthetically dominant when it comes to learning.

> Most messages are auditory. Make yours more visual and kinesthetic.

You can see why it is vital to address all three learning channels every time you communicate to an audience.

SWITCHING CHANNELS THROUGHOUT YOUR MESSAGE

If you do not pay attention to your audience's preferences, you may throw away your opportunity to make an impact. That's why it is critical to integrate elements of all three learning styles into the delivery of your presentation. After all, you cannot afford to neglect those in your audience who favor a different learning channel. Using multiple channels also helps the old brain stay alert.

The best way to keep your audience engaged and to make sure that a large majority of people comprehend your message is to vary your presentation in order to address all three learning styles. If you only make use of PowerPoint slides with lots of text, you technically limit your appeal to the auditory channel of your audience. This makes

MOST BUSINESSES TODAY
BROADCAST ONE CHANNEL ONLY!

Tell me, how many times have you
- seen PowerPoint presentations that squeeze sentence after sentence onto each slide?
- been bored to death with a speaker who rambles without giving a demo, sharing a story, or presenting a strong visual?

If your answer to the above is "too many to count," here is the reason: Business or technical presentations today primarily use the auditory channel. Technology companies in particular have a strong tendency to sell their solutions using only this channel.

Why? Many people who are tech savvy tend to primarily use their new brain, the part responsible for thinking and logic, so they feel more comfortable explaining the solutions they sell in a linear, rational, feature-centric way.

your message more difficult for visual or kinesthetic learners to process, and it does not help keep the old brain awake.

Take the example of the Linux Open Source Model (Figure 18-1). Can you determine which channel is used to convey the mesage, the visual or the auditory channel?

The Linux Open Source Model

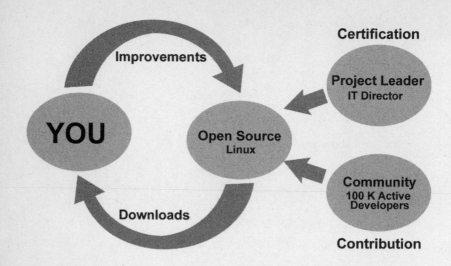

FIGURE 18-1

Most people think that a diagram like Figure 18-1 is visual and therefore helps the visual learner. IT IS NOT! A diagram may be a better way of organizing written information, but because people have to read it in order to understand it, it cannot be learned through the visual channel. It is still primarily auditory.

Now let's look at another example from the complex world of technology. This diagram (Figure 18-2), although it does contain text, is primarily visual. The puzzle shape carries significance, which is best understood visually. The puzzle itself is a strong visual metaphor. You immediately comprehend how each element relates to each other via the connecting centerpiece.

Visual supports make a huge impact on any audience. Printed ads, for example, primarily use the visual channel because advertisers

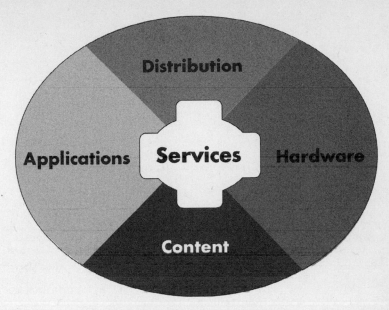

FIGURE 18-2

know that since images make a direct impact on the old brain, readers will get the message much faster and more effectively.

Recent data published by the 3M Meeting Management Institute illustrates the value of true visual information:

- Retention increases from 14 to 38 percent when listeners see, as well as listen to, a presentation.
- Group consensus is 21 percent higher in meetings with visual aids.
- The time required to communicate a concept is reduced by 40 percent with the use of effective visuals.

When presenting, resist the impulse to talk about your solution or to simply list its features. Spend some time identifying powerful ways to make your presentations more visual or kinesthetic to keep the decision-maker, the old brain, awake and informed.

LEARNING CHANNELS
IN CURRENT ADVERTISING

Have you ever noticed that most clothing ads are highly visual and use little or no text? What is the pain of people who buy jeans? With so many choices, it comes down to the fact that they really just want to look "cool."

How do clothing ads prove the gain to their potential customers? The models in the ad are typically young, attractive, and hip. You respond because, thanks to a visual and concrete message, your primitive old brain believes that you, too, can look or feel like the

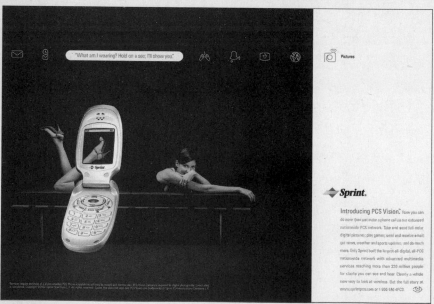

FIGURE 18-3

model who is wearing that certain brand of cool jeans if you buy them.

Notice that clothing ads typically do not try to sell you on the quality of the fabric, the number of pockets, the copper rivets, or the zipper. They target what they know is consumers' number one pain: our desire to look cool. In a one-page ad, with limited space

FIGURE 18-4

and time, a visual grabber is the best way to get the attention of the old brain.

In the ad for cellular phone service (Figure 18-3), Sprint visually demonstrates the gain provided by their new phones where users can literally see and send a visual response.

In another example, because their target audience is very specific, note how an advertiser enhances a message by addressing a learning channel other than the visual one (Figure 18-4).

BMW discovered that a large number of their prospects belonged to a group known as Audiophiles: people who love music and demand very high-end high-fidelity systems. Undoubtedly, people who read stereo magazines tend to be more auditory. The visual in this ad shows a barrage of stereo speakers: tangible objects that the reader can easily identify with. Notice how the ad copy also appeals to the auditory channel.

WHICH LEARNING CHANNEL DO YOU FAVOR?

Try this: read the following sentence and quickly count the number of *f*s it contains. When you are finished counting the *f*s, write down the number you found.

It is only after a thorough evaluation of the prospect's pain that the astute seller will demonstrate the proven value of her uniqueness. She will do so with the impact of a grabber that uses the three learning channels of her audience.

How many *f*s did you count? The correct answer is five, yet most auditory people will only find one. It typically takes auditory people several tries before they find all five *f*s because when they read the word *of*, they hear the *v* sound, which does not include an *f*.

Now let's take a simple test to figure out your preferred learning channel. First, just relax and take a deep breath. In a few moments, I'm going to give you a specific word. Try to remember the first thing that comes to your mind when you read the word. The word is . . . (turn the page):

bell

Was your first instinct to . . . hear a bell? see a bell? feel or touch a bell? This simple exercise can give a first clue as to which channel you favor most.

In past presentations, have you equally used all three learning channels to reach your audience, or did you only use the auditory channel?

TIPS ON ACCESSING ALL THREE CHANNELS

Here are examples of what you can do to address the various learning styles, which will prevent the old brain from sinking to the bottom of the attention/retention curve:

- *Tell stories.* Stories are conveyed with words, yet when well-told, they create sensory impressions that use all three learning channels. The old brain is made to believe that the story really happened to him or her.
- *Use good visuals.* Look at your slides. Are they just a repeat of what you are saying, or even worse, are you just reading them? Or are your slides creating a higher level of understanding by providing real visual information?

- *Involve the audience.* Having the audience participate will make them use their kinesthetic channel. Ask them questions, have them raise their hands to signal whether they agree or disagree, let them talk, let them create exercises, let them touch an object such as a prop, or let them perform a demo themselves. Give them positive reinforcement when they participate. All this will appeal to their kinesthetic channel and, ultimately, to their old brain.

Another easy but effective way to involve the different styles is to use words that evoke each channel. For instance, "Do you see what I mean?" works great for a visual person. "I hear you," works better for an auditory person, and "It feels good, doesn't it?" is effective for kinesthetic learners. Vary your language to keep the old brain awake in addition to using props or visuals.

One final note: do you remember the best question you should ask to receive positive public feedback during your close—"What do you think?" You will notice that this sentence is very neutral and doesn't favor any particular learning channel. You wouldn't want to close a presentation by asking, "Do you see the benefits of our solution?" to a prospect who is primarily auditory. By keeping your closing question neutral, especially if you have intentionally addressed all three learning styles throughout your message, you will have a higher percentage of your audience who can either *see* your point, *hear* your message, or *move* toward accepting your claims!

WHAT TO REMEMBER

Although all people use the three learning channels—visual, auditory, and kinesthetic—everybody has a favorite one. To address your audience effectively, vary your learning channels. Your message is apt to be primarily auditory: make it more visual and kinesthetic by using real pictures, props, exercises, mini-dramas, and stories.

19

IMPACT BOOSTER #6:
STORIES

*Persuasion always works better when the persuaded
is not aware that he or she is being influenced.*
~DR. JOSEPH LEDOUX, PROFESSOR OF
NEUROSCIENCE, CENTER FOR NEURAL SCIENCE, NYU

Do you remember the different types of grabbers we discussed way
back in chapter 8? Techniques like mini-dramas and wordplays?
Stories also make for good grabbers. In fact, stories are so effective
that they should be mandatory in every presentation. If the delivery
of your message involves some form of face-to-face communication,
you should use stories as a strategic tool to influence your audience.

In addition to grabbers, stories can and should be used in the development of your Message Building Blocks such as your big picture, your proofs of gain, or handling objections. In fact, the best messages are those developed from beginning to end as a complete and compelling story. How is it possible that such an innocuous action as telling a story can have such tremendous effect on your audience?

Once again, it's a play for the old brain. We are grown-up, rational people, yet when we see a movie, we often experience strong emotions that make us sad, mad, or even move us to tears. We know it's only fiction: 100 percent made in Hollywood. The hero didn't really die; that little kid did not lose his parents—yet we still cry. Our new brain is well-aware that nothing bad really happened, yet the real boss, the old brain, with its primitive level of intelligence, does not differentiate between reality and a well-told story. Thus, the old brain releases a flood of hormones that trigger our lachrymal glands and other physiological responses such as a tight throat and watering eyes.

Good stories have more impact on the old brain and our subconscious than any rational fact. To create a good story, it is essential to

- Create a world of sensory impressions using visual, auditory, and kinesthetic clues that will fool the old brain into believing that what you told really happened.
- Clearly connect the story you are telling with the world of your client: why should they care?
- Make sure your story really has a point or a punch line.

So why is it so rare to hear good stories? "The real problem is that nobody knows how to tell a story. And what's worse, nobody knows that they don't know how to tell a story!" observes Jerry Weissman, an expert presenter and coach to CEOs of top companies like Inuit and Yahoo! in his book *Presenting to Win: The Art of Telling Your Story*.

Remember that the old brain is visual. Though you may believe that your PowerPoint presentation represents a good story, the reality is that it often looks more like the Yellow Pages—a lot of text—rather than a good Hollywood movie that would please your audience.

> The old brain cannot tell the difference between reality and a well-told story.

If you have kids, you probably already know the difference between a good story and one that is not so good. If your kid leaves in the middle of your story, it's a good sign that you need to improve on your technique.

The impact of a story depends on two factors:

- your content
- your delivery

You must excel in both if you really expect to compel listeners to buy from you today as opposed to tomorrow.

On the content side, this book provides you with a canvas to create your own story, starting with the pain of your audience, followed by your unique claims and the supporting proofs of gain: a solid plan for maximum impact on your audience.

On the delivery side, your credibility will add to the impact of your story. Notice how this book reviewed your Creativity, your Fearlessness, your Passion, your Integrity, your Accessibility, and finally, your

Expressiveness—words, voice, and body language—as the main areas that will reinforce or diminish your impact. In fact, the best stories are true stories that really happened either to you or someone close to you, because when you tell that story with the passion of an active witness, your story will become easily believable by your audience's old brain.

Either you were born a great storyteller, or you can learn it. Many good books out there can help. Better yet, take a drama or speech class.

Now, before we finish, let me tell you one last story:

One of our clients was preparing to deliver a compelling presentation to an international buying committee. The stakes were high: be on a short list of three selected vendors and win a contract valued at over 50 million dollars, or lose and see several million dollars of annual business disappear instantly.

When the company approached us, the executive team was planning a standard technical PowerPoint presentation which, though it would make them look professional, would surely fail to make their presentation memorable or to differentiate them from other, larger competitors. There was just one solution: design a presentation that would impact their prospects' old brain. The PowerPoint had to go.

Their VP of global accounts, Heinz Stumpe, was an incredible individual whose charisma and extraordinary energy were simply not well-served by an illuminated screen with lots of text upstaging him. Though he had over twenty years of experience in the business closing hundreds of high-level deals using PowerPoint slides, we challenged him to give them up and tell a personal story instead—something that had nothing to do with technology—to deliver his vital points with maximum impact.

Heinz, a former two-time karate world champion, rose to the occasion with incredible style. While most of the competitors for this deal were large billion-dollar companies involving multiple business segments, his company was the only one 100 percent focused on the line of products for which the bid was staged.

At the start of his newly improved presentation, Heinz displayed the logos of his main competitors; then he immediately turned off the computer and faced the audience. He explained that the main difference between the competition and his company was that the competitors were not focused on one business sector. So, regardless of their size, they did not have the same level of experience in one discipline and would never achieve the same effectiveness Heinz and his company could provide.

"When I teach karate," Heinz began, "some of the students at the advanced levels start feeling pretty confident when they get their black belt. It's a very high level, and it takes lots of hard work to get there. So they look at me, the instructor, wearing my own black belt, and they start to make comparisons. They feel they've finally arrived and that now they're in the same league as the teachers. They take such pride in breaking boards or bricks with rapid and powerful hits, kicks, and punches.

"Now, there are several levels, called 'dans,' within the black belt itself," Heinz continued, "and what the kids don't know is that what separates a black belt at a high-level dan—say seventh or eighth, which is world championship level—from someone who just got their first black belt and is still at the first dan, is years and years of focus and experience. Literally thousands of hours of practice and focus have gone into achieving that experience. There is no shortcut that will get them to that level. Only years of effort, experience, and focus can do it.

"The first exercise I give the students in my classes is not just to break a brick, but to break a brick with a one-inch punch. They are usually game at first, trying every way they can to break the brick by simply placing their fingertips on the brick and striking it as hard as they can. The problem is, with a one-inch punch, there's not much room to get momentum."

Heinz approached the table where the buying team sat and demonstrated the way to place the hand, vertically above the table, fingers pointing straight down with his fingertips resting lightly on the table.

Suddenly, catching everyone off guard, Heinz delivered a swift, extraordinarily powerful impact to the table by quickly bending his fingers and making a fist, which hit the table with a violent sound and alarming tremble.

"It's not just about having knowledge in a particular field; it's not even just about the power of focus," he said. "It's about the power of years of experience of working on one thing with tremendous focus."

The committee was still processing the rush of emotions as Heinz delivered his main point. The presentation was to become the best the prospect committee saw, and they talked about it for months. After a series of carefully thought-out and well-rehearsed events—including powerful stories that would impact the old brain—Heinz's company won the deal.

Tell stories. Good stories make a concept visual and tangible. They can make it personal, show contrast, and generate powerful emotion. In short, stories speak a powerful language that reaches not only the heart but also the old brain.

WHAT TO REMEMBER

Stories are a powerful way to grab attention and stir up emotion. For a good story, create a world with sensory details that make listeners feel it really happened, clearly connect your story to your client's world, and make sure that it has a clear point or punch line. Learn how to tell good stories, and then tell them.

IMPACT BOOSTER #7:
LESS IS MORE

Let your discourse with men of business
be short and comprehensive.

~GEORGE WASHINGTON, FIRST US PRESIDENT

Is there anything else you can do to maximize your selling probability? The answer is yes: make your message shorter.

Imagine you are selling a product that has one hundred individual
features. These one hundred features could easily be converted into
thirty benefits, which in turn, could cure ten of your prospects' pain.
Isn't it obvious, then, that you should sell these ten cures?

NO! That was a trick question. You should focus only on the top three, or even simply the number one benefit that would cure your prospect's number one pain. Why? Because your prospect's old brain likes to keep it simple.

Your survival brain likes to see the best choice at a glance because the time and energy required for analysis tend to cloud issues and slow things down. It tends to think thoughts like, "If I buy a product that is more complex, the probability that something will go wrong is higher. If this vendor is selling a solution that offers so many options, maybe I just need a simpler, less expensive solution."

So, instead of giving your prospects all the reasons why they should buy from you, just focus your message on your one to three claims that address their top pain.

"Less is more" means you must remove anything from your message that has no direct value for your prospects. Make every element in your message count. Go for quality instead of quantity. Look at your message from the viewpoint of your prospects and ask yourself: "So what? Will this piece of information help me make a buying decision?" If the answer is no, remove it.

Here is another important question to ask yourself: "Is the information I am giving absolutely necessary in order for my prospect to understand the bigger picture or in order for him or her to make a buying decision?"

Is the information you are providing needed for your prospect's decision to buy? If not, then you are telling, not selling. Telling is often necessary, but you should consider passing on training information in a written document that can be studied later, not in a face-to-face meeting or on the phone. Telling does NOT equal selling. Never turn a selling event into a telling event!

Impact Booster #7: Less Is More

Before you finalize your presentation, review all your Message Building Blocks and condense your message until you can no longer remove anything without losing value. Don't be afraid to remove complete portions of your message if they don't pass the "So what?" test. The ultimate test is to make sure that you are not adding slides to help yourself remember what to say!

If you apply the principles of neuromarketing, you will quickly realize that, by simplifying the content, your existing messages and presentations can be delivered in about half the time, while your impact will increase tremendously.

Remember Agnes and the mini-drama about Marco of Venezuela? With her creative message focused on her prospect's pain, she was able to sell them on her message in about three minutes. Prospects will appreciate it if you only take thirty minutes of their time for a presentation that was supposed to last one hour, not to mention that the remaining minutes may provide you with valuable time to handle objections before you go.

Recently, we coached one of our clients to fine-tune what was meant to be a two-hour presentation down to a very lean, but very powerful, forty minutes.

They resisted at first, feeling they should take advantage of the full two-hour time slot that was allotted to them, and not wanting to have less face time than the competing presentations. What they found in the long run was that after their absolutely fabulous forty minutes, the client spent the rest of the time just talking to them, providing feedback and information. It was, in the end, a much more valuable use of their time than talking "at" the client for the full two hours as their competitors did.

Best of all, their decision was validated when the client said, "Your presentation is the only one we wish had been longer."

Have you been guilty of overkill? Be honest. Neuromarketing starts with attention to detail. Review and re-review every element in your message to make it as effective and tight as it can be.

WHAT TO REMEMBER

More words do not equal more impact. Telling does NOT equal selling. As you get ready to deliver your message, remove anything from your message that has no value for your prospects. Think impact or emotion rather than quantity.

WHAT TO REMEMBER FOR THE SEVEN IMPACT BOOSTERS:

1. Use the word **You** frequently.
2. **Maximize your Credibility** with these traits:
   - Creativity
   - Fearlessness
   - Passion
   - Integrity
   - Accessibility
   - Expressiveness.
3. Use **Contrast** everywhere.
4. **Generate Emotion**.
5. Vary **Learning Styles**.
6. Tell good **Stories**.
7. **Less Is More**: cut down your presentation to what is truly essential.

CONCLUSION

MARKETING IS DEAD; LONG LIVE NEUROMARKETING

Congratulations! You have finished leaning about the most effective ways to increase your influence in all your sales, communication, and even in your personal life. By understanding the "buy buttons" in your prospects' brains, you will not only enjoy the tremendous power of creating and delivering powerful messages that influence people, but you will also recognize how others influence you by speaking to your own old brain.

In these pages you have discovered a powerful framework for a completely new way of looking at selling and influencing based on the newest brain research. The world's best salespeople, presenters, politicians, and influencers practice these techniques intuitively, and now you have learned why and how their methods work: they target the true decision-maker, the old brain.

Why a Simplified Model?

Much of the technology used by neuroscientists today is out of reach for most companies. For example, most will not be able to afford an MRI study to find out what color packaging will most likely sell. This is one reason for the value of the old brain theory. By learning its simplified model, anyone in marketing, sales, or advertising can expect to get more effective, predictable, and repeatable results. In addition, restaurant owners, lawyers, real estate brokers, dentists, architects, contractors, politicians, bakers, and others may have better things to do than to learn the art of selling, yet their success often lies more in their selling abilities than in their own trade expertise. This model can alleviate the natural human fear about selling that many of us have.

Bridging the Gap between Sales and Marketing

One of the strongest benefits of neuromarketing is that it provides a common language for sales and marketing functions. In many companies, sales and marketing departments don't share a common platform to communicate, and the business pays the severe price of a house divided. Indeed, each discipline has different objectives and perceptions of how to cooperate and align for success. Because the functions are separated, messages are diluted, distorted, or—worse—ignored.

Conclusion

In market conditions that are tougher than ever, the search is heating up for a way to bridge this damaging split and to ensure that valuable time and resources are not wasted. With neuromarketing, sales and marketing functions can finally coalesce around four simple steps:

- Diagnose the customers' Pain (not just the wishes, wants, or needs).
- Differentiate the company's Claims (more concrete than positioning).
- Demonstrate the Gain (prove that the value proposition is the core of selling).
- Deliver the message to the Old Brain (help people understand and trigger a decision or closing).

Our neuromarketing model offers a rich library of techniques that are instrumental in the creation and delivery of your messages. In short, your messages reach the part of the brain that decides. By introducing them in your activities, you will automatically create synergies between sales, marketing, post-sales, customer service, and any other departments that are communicating with your customers. As an individual, your mastery of all these concepts will make you much more valuable to your clients.

How can you afford to miss an opportunity to reach the old brain of your audiences in such a consistent and powerful way?

SELLING TO THE OLD BRAIN IN EVERYDAY LIFE

This section describes how you can follow the four steps in common yet critical everyday sales situations, including:

- Targeting Your Prospects
- Designing Print Ads
- Producing Web Sites
- Creating E-mails
- Leaving Voicemails
- Delivering Speeches
- Giving Presentations
- Getting a Job

Targeting Your Prospects

Imagine you are looking at introducing a new product that can appeal to multiple groups of prospects. You need to focus on one group or cluster to maximize your chances of success. How can you best decide which cluster is the most likely to adopt your solution?

STEP 1: DIAGNOSE THE PAIN
First, cluster your potential prospects into groups with similar pain. Since this may require extensive marketing research and great knowledge of your market, it often helps to do this as a team with the contributions of all relevant departments: marketing, sales, technical experts, PR, and executives. For each cluster, evaluate the pain factor as a number from 0 to 1: where 0 is no pain at all, and where 1 is the most intense, urgent, and acute pain.

STEP 2: DIFFERENTIATE YOUR CLAIMS
For each cluster, choose and rate your claims. These claims should solve the main pain. Rate them from 0 to 1: where 0 means your claims are totally false, they don't address the pain, and they are unsubstantiated, and where 1 means your claims are perfectly aligned with the pain, they are totally unique to you, and you can prove them.

STEP 3: DEMONSTRATE THE GAIN
Now for each cluster, you should rate the proof factor of each of your value statements. Do you have strong customer stories with similar pain, or can you use only some marketing data or your vision? Rate

your proofs with a factor from 0 to 1: where 0 means you cannot prove any gain for your prospects, and where 1 means your gain is maximum and you can bring an irrefutable proof.

Now, calculate your Cluster Attractiveness:

$$\textbf{(Pain) x (Claim) x (Proven Gain)}$$
$$\textbf{= Your Cluster Attractiveness}$$

The higher values of Cluster Attractiveness will indicate the low-hanging fruit, those groups of prospects that will be easiest for you to close.

After you have found the most likely candidates, evaluate each cluster's size, either in number of prospects or in dollar amount, as shown in the table.

Now you can calculate your Cluster Opportunity:

$$\textbf{(Pain) x (Claim) x (Proven Gain) x (Cluster Size)}$$
$$\textbf{= Your Cluster Opportunity}$$

$$\text{or}$$

$$\textbf{Your Cluster Opportunity =}$$
$$\textbf{(Your Cluster Attractiveness) x (Cluster Size)}$$

In the following example, we assumed the pain, the claims, the proven gain, and the cluster size for each of the four clusters. Then, the cluster attractiveness and the cluster opportunity were calculated using the above formulas.

This approach gives you a simple way to combine the size and value of your market with your strength in each segment. It also helps you to avoid two of the major strategic mistakes of many of today's marketing strategies: either always going after the biggest cluster, or deciding on target markets based on only some of your strengths. Those approaches fail to take into account other factors, such as the market resistance you may face in that cluster.

Cluster Attractiveness & Opportunity				
	Cluster A	**Cluster B**	**Cluster C**	**Cluster D**
PAIN	0.8	0.90	0.6	0.8
CLAIM	0.7	.90	.95	0.8
Proven GAIN	1	0.5	0.6	0.8
Your Cluster Attractiveness	0.56	0.405	0.342	0.512
Cluster Size in $M	50	100	150	120
Your Cluster Opportunity	28	40.5	51.3	61.44

The marketing strategy you choose will depend on your situation. In this example, if you were looking for your first customers, you might choose Cluster A, where you have the strongest competitive position. If you were pressed by time and decided you wanted to close a small number of prospects quickly, then you should choose the cluster where your Cluster Attractiveness is the highest. In this case it would also be Cluster A.

If you were going after the biggest cluster, you would be targeting the prospects from Cluster C. Although this choice might be a large potential market, it will be difficult for you to sell in that market with a Cluster Attractiveness of only 34.2 percent.

Choosing your marketing focus based solely on the amount of pain of the various clusters would push you toward the prospects in Cluster B. These prospects might be more eager to buy, but they would also lead you to difficulties. Although the situation might work for a mass market with shotgun advertising for a low-priced product, your proven gain in that market is only 0.5. That means your Cluster Attractiveness and your Cluster Opportunity in this cluster are both quite low.

The best long-term approach would be to choose Cluster D, the cluster with your highest Cluster Opportunity.

This type of analysis gives you great strategic flexibility. You may pick different markets at different times in the product life cycle or depending on your resources. But you will always have a simple yet powerful tool to use for your marketing decisions.

YOUR PRINT ADS

STEP 1: DIAGNOSE THE PAIN
In printed ads, 75 percent of your time should be spent on this step. If you assume the wrong pain, you will end up promoting the wrong gain to your prospects, effectively sabotaging the sale before it ever gets off the ground.

Find your prospects' needs through appropriate marketing research, prospect interviews, and an effective analysis of your knowledge about the market. List the main areas of pain, and then focus on the top pain.

Since the headline is worth more than 50 percent of the power of a print ad, it should be a grabber that deals both with the pain and the relief brought by your solution.

STEP 2: DIFFERENTIATE YOUR CLAIMS
Choose one claim (or two, maximum), and then focus your entire message around the pain that can be cured by your specific claim.

STEP 3: DEMONSTRATE THE GAIN
This is the most difficult challenge in printed ads: to prove the value without using a lot of text. The proof of gain should be clearly illustrated in the picture.

STEP 4: DELIVER TO THE OLD BRAIN
This step is where you should spend most of the remaining 25 percent of your time. Creativity will be key. Printed ads are usually just a grabber or a big picture; on one single page, it is difficult to insert any additional Message Building Blocks. There simply isn't enough space.

A big picture is usually the most effective way to reach the old brain because it is highly visual. When it links to a short, punchy headline, your impact is maximized. In fact, a picture used as a grabber in a print ad often doubles as your diagnostic; the reader should feel that she or he identifies with her or his pain in that picture. Then, you can discuss or show relief to the pain that is portrayed.

When presenting your big picture, consider using contrast. Portray your prospects' lives as they exist without your product today, and then their future with your product tomorrow. Make sure about 80 percent of the ad is a picture: minimize the amount of text since people often don't take time to read. You'll only have a few seconds to get to their old brain, so make it count: make it visual!

Be sure you are targeting the audience that will read that specific magazine or newspaper. Make the message totally tailored to the pain those readers have in common.

All examples of print ads featured in this book follow these rules. Two or three have even managed to add their claims. The proof of gain is usually included in the big picture. Remember the CareerBuilder Network ad about a man trying to catch a Red-Spotted Grouper fish? Often print ads do not develop their value proposition; they simply focus on grabbing your attention. Since it's difficult in a one-page ad to close the sale on the spot, their objective is to get you interested enough to take some sort of action such as calling for information or checking their Web site.

In a print ad, you often have enough space to emphasize the prospects' pain. Make sure you are impacting the old brain by making their current situation without your solution look painful!

YOUR WEB SITE

STEP 1: DIAGNOSE THE PAIN

Here, again, you should know exactly who your target audience is and what the objectives of your Web site are. For example, is the purpose of your Web site to attract investors, to attract prospects, to attract new employees, or to motivate your current employees? The top pain of each of these targets is not the same.

Assuming the main objective is to attract prospects, it is important that you classify your prospects in groups that have similar pain. The old brain is not interested in reading about somebody else's pain. Therefore, you may want to create different URL entry points in your Web site depending on the prospects' main pain. If you find your prospects belong to three main clusters with distinct areas of pain, you may want to consider creating three distinct parts of your Web site to address each group separately.

STEP 2: DIFFERENTIATE YOUR CLAIMS

Choose two or three claims. Then for each cluster of prospects, focus all your messages around the pain that is related to these claims.

STEP 3: DEMONSTRATE THE GAIN

Typically, a Web site offers a good opportunity to develop your proofs of gain. So, for each cluster, develop your value matrix and use the strongest proofs you can present. For example, using a customer case study along with a picture, and then quoting your customer's strong value statement, will have great impact on the old brain because it becomes tangible and personal.

A Web site is versatile. You should use as little text as possible in your opening message; you can provide links to pages of written details, pictures, sound, and so forth for those who want it. Include audio or video whenever possible, and sprinkle in any new features provided by the latest versions of Internet browsers. Well-designed Web sites are the one area of marketing where you can include infinite detail without boring people who only want the basics.

STEP 4: DELIVER TO THE OLD BRAIN

For each cluster, use a grabber that makes your prospect re-experience their main pain. Use a big picture that visually shows how you will impact their world. Develop your claims and repeat them throughout your pages.

Go into the details of your proofs of gain, making sure not to concentrate on you and your company, but instead on how you can improve your prospects' life financially, strategically, and personally.

Of course, you will still want to provide a section of your Web site that talks about you, but do not place this section ahead of the pain and your claims. Make it easy for your prospects to find the nuggets; do not bury your strong proofs of gain under twenty clicks.

YOUR E-MAILS

Even the simplest form of communication can be effectively done, or it can head straight for the cyberspace trash can. Every form of contact from you should be well-thought-out.

STEP 1: DIAGNOSE THE PAIN

First, you need to obtain the name and exact function of the person you are trying to reach. Remember, the old brain is very self-centered, so most people don't even read e-mails that look like a mass mailing.

A search engine like Google can give you background information on the industry, trade associations, and competitors. At your prospect's Web site, you can learn about the company so you can better assess the pain and customize your grabber. Are they making their numbers? Did they go through any acquisitions or right-sizing? Did they launch a new product recently? What does the press say about them? How much of this really impacts the person you are trying to reach? For example, if you are contacting the VP of sales and the company has not made its numbers for the last several quarters, be prepared to offer this person something that can increase their revenue!

STEP 2: DIFFERENTIATE YOUR CLAIMS
At this point, you will most likely not need to state your claims. If you do start to introduce your claims this early in the process, make sure they are indeed unique and that you can back them up with strong proofs of gain later.

STEP 3: DEMONSTRATE THE GAIN
In a short e-mail, you will not have many opportunities to prove the gain. However, the core of your message should be about the benefit of your product for them. In a postscript, you also can include a quote from a prospect that gives you a strong testimonial for a gain statement. To further increase your e-mail's impact, you could creatively replace this quote with an audio, or even better, a visual video clip of a customer giving testimonial in person. Most e-mail software now supports this feature. When you record the testimonial, make sure both the voice and body language convey a positive message.

STEP 4: DELIVER TO THE OLD BRAIN
Again, as in print ads, the time a prospect will give an e-mail is extremely short. Your grabber will be vital. You need a subject line

that makes them want to open your e-mail. Inside, you should also include a visual graphic: a contrasted big picture would be best as long as it opens quickly in all browsers.

Because you have neither your voice nor your body to convey your energy, carefully choose every word you use. Make your message as personal as possible to appeal to the self-centered aspect of the old brain. One simple thing you can do is copy and paste an image of their logo into the e-mail.

Develop your proofs of gain in as few words as possible and repeat your claims at least twice. Remember, less is more: make it half a page or less. Statistically, if the message doesn't fit within the screen, many people will not scroll to see what's remaining.

Close with a clear objective.

Example: Let's assume you are trying to get an appointment for a one-hour meeting with an executive at a large software company called IBN (International Business Network). This person doesn't know you, but you are convinced they could use your product. You learn from their Web site that their revenues are declining. You've heard through your network that the morale of the sales force is low. You have previously closed a sale with their main competitor, a company called GNS (Global Networking Solutions), and GNS has just reported a record quarter. Your product is a CRM (Customer Relation Management) tool, and the name of your company is CloseProspects.

You can obtain IBN's actual revenue curve and their logo from their Web site. This is an easy way of making your message personal and introducing a short but effective financial value proof. Don't forget to use color in your text.

Here is an example of an "old brain-friendly" email you could write:

Subject line: _____

Dear Mr. Smith,

What if you could turn revenues from _____?

What if your sales force could close more deals and build relationships with your customers?

You will find that many software companies like yours have seen a significant jump in revenues immediately after implementing our CRM software. How? By:

- Closing more prospects
- Staying closer to their customers

Sharen Tilst, VP of sales at GNS, commented, "With the new software from CloseProspects, our salespeople have closed 25 percent more business, and our support people can finally claim that they truly are able to maintain close contact with our existing customers. Our satisfaction ratios have jumped 47 percent."

If you want to increase your own sales and hear your customers singing your praises, call John Goodman at 555-1212.

> With your success in mind,
> John Goodman
> CRM Expert
> CloseProspects.com

Your Voicemails

Do you see voicemail as a "black hole," where your messages go in and nothing comes out?! Always be prepared to reach your target live, but if you don't, leave a powerful voicemail so you don't waste a golden opportunity.

Step 1: Diagnose the pain

Find out as much as you can about the prospect before calling.

Step 2: Differentiate your claims

You do not need to state your claims, as you will most likely not have enough time to state them . . . or the prospect will not remember them later.

Step 3: Demonstrate the gain

Make a short statement of your proofs of gain. Be sure to use specific, concrete language. Depending on whom the voicemail is addressed to, a financial gain statement might be the strongest.

Step 4: Deliver to the old brain

Do not pick up the phone before writing down what you will say! Prepare two scenarios:
- One for voicemail
- One for a live call if your prospect answers the phone

Typically, voicemails should be very short: twenty or thirty seconds, maximum. If you start your voicemail with your name and the prospect doesn't know you, you take the risk that they may erase the message before listening to the whole thing. In today's time-starved environment, many prospects do not have the time of day for what they may perceive to be yet another average sales call.

So, basically, you have time for a short grabber and a brief proof of gain. Close with your contact information. Less is more, so remove every unnecessary word.

Your only highlighter is your voice, so practice, practice, practice before you actually call. Pay careful attention to your tone, the speed at which you talk, and the use of your "best friend" voice.

Example: Using the same scenario as we did in the e-mail, here is what you could say using a short financial proof of gain:

Mr. Smith, what if you could increase revenues by 25 percent? Yes, you can close more deals by building relationships with your customers. That is what happened at GNS. Three months after installing the CloseProspects CRM product, GNS reported a 12 percent profit increase while their customer satisfaction ratio jumped 47 percent. To find out how you, too, can achieve the same results, call me, John Goodman, at CloseProspects: 555-1212.

Here, again, you could greatly enhance the impact of this message if you played a prepared, short (ten-second) audio testimonial from Sharen Tilst herself, saying, "My name is Sharen Tilst, and I'm VP of sales at GNS. Three months after installing CloseProspects, we reported a 12 percent profit increase and our customer satisfaction ratios jumped 47 percent." Remember, a customer story is good; a customer testimonial is even better.

Your Speeches

We have discussed different strategies, language, and body language for your presentations. Here is a quick summary.

Step 1: Diagnose the Pain

Find the most common pain of the attendees in the audience. Stay away from generalities, and be as specific as possible about the pain. Select the most acute pain. Ask your audience if they agree with your diagnostic, and identify a few head movements as a "yes."

Step 2: Differentiate Your Claims

Choose claims that correlate with the pain you have identified.

Step 3: Demonstrate the Gain

Choose the proofs that are the strongest and most relevant to your audience as a group.

Step 4: Deliver to the Old Brain

Use all the Message Building Blocks described in this book: grabber, big picture, claims, proofs of gain, handling objections, and closing.

You may insert your credentials into your speech, but preferably, do it after your grabber. Your introduction should establish your credibility so the audience is open to receiving your information as an expert in your field. Make it short but informative, precise, visual, and personal. Tell them why it's relevant for them to pay attention to you.

In his book *Leading Out Loud*, author Terry Pearce gives a great example of the best way to deliver credentials. Terry tells of the case of a young professional who was introduced to a business audience simply as an "environmental consultant" who would speak on the topic of "urban conservation." The consultant was prepared to supplement whatever introduction he received and proceeded to elaborate for the audience.

"I have been extremely fortunate to have spent most of my life educating myself for my work," he said. "I have spent almost twenty-five years in schools and over thirty years in the outdoors. I've traveled from the Arctic Ocean to the equator, climbed some of the highest peaks in Europe, and trekked through the jungles of Borneo. As an environmental consultant for six years, I've visited more garbage dumps than I care to remember. I've been involved with oil spills off the coast of Alaska and train wrecks in densely populated urban areas. My conclusion from all these experiences? We are not living a sustainable existence."

Go for impact. Remember, the way you deliver is key to getting and holding attention, and making the sale.

Keep the room cold and well-lit. This will prevent your audience's old brain from idling too quickly. Use real pictures, video clips, and/or audiotapes. Involve the audience. Minimize the amount of text. Use key words, but "tell" the content using all the techniques that make great selling events. Use variety in color, in voice, and in movements. If other presenters use PowerPoint, try using a flip chart if the room is not too big. Make it an absolute "must" to use at least one prop and several stories.

Move from behind the podium, and use as much space as possible. Address the audience directly and individually, establishing and maintaining eye contact with the people in the front rows. You should look, feel, and sound different from the other speakers—yet you should look, feel, and sound similar and friendly to your audience.

Rehearse, rehearse, and rehearse. You don't have to learn your text word for word, but you should be able to make your presentation without reading. DO NOT READ your text at all costs, and do not repeat what is already written on your slides. Your slides should support your presentation, not replace it.

Remember, the old brain is much more sensitive to your energy than to a spreadsheet, regardless of how good the numbers look.

Your Presentations

In today's world, it almost always requires three to four people to say "yes" before you get the order or commitment. If you are doing your job efficiently as a salesperson, you need to meet all four decision-influencers. Giving a formal presentation of your product is a very effective way of reaching the whole group at once.

We each have the same twenty-four hours in a day. The biggest difference between those who are successful and those who are not is the way they make use of their time. I suggest that you focus your energy on your top accounts.

Invest a lot of time preparing. It's better to deliver one presentation a week and close 30 percent than to do two presentations a week and close only 10 percent. For big-ticket items, there are few "one-call closes." The objective of your presentations should be to close or to get a commitment to move the sales process forward.

If your diagnostic is correct and the prospect acknowledges it, if you present your unique claims and back them up with solid proofs of gain, and if you demonstrate beyond any doubt that you are the ONLY solution that can solve their pain, then why would they further delay a decision? Every passing day would cause them to lose money. Bring this to the attention of their old brain—which should be highly sensitive to that fact!

STEP 1: DIAGNOSE THE PAIN

Find out as much as you can about the pain of your target group. No two prospects have exactly the same pain. The more specific you can be about their own pain, the faster you will reach their old brain.

Ideally, you should have each prospect acknowledge your diagnostic of their pain before the presentation. This way you will know for sure that what you are selling is a cure to their pain.

Go to your prospect's Web site, read their newsletters, talk to people internally, find a pretext to set up a short one-on-one meeting prior to the big presentation to learn about or confirm their pain. Tell them, for example, that you are preparing for the presentation you have set up in two weeks, and you would like to confirm the pain you are assuming they have so that this presentation really zeros in on their most important issues and is a good investment of their time. It is smart to get early "buy-in" from each key decision-maker before a general meeting.

In fact, you should invest most of your energy setting up these one-on-one meetings prior to D-day so that on D-day your sales presentation is 100 percent selling and 0 percent telling. D-day should be reserved for proving the value of your claims to solve their top pain.

Remember, the biggest issue is making sure you are going after the right pain. One of the most common mistakes is to prepare a presentation that attempts to solve a pain that the prospect doesn't even have. The key to successful formal presentations is to make sure your prospect has acknowledged the pain that you have diagnosed prior to the meeting.

STEP 2: DIFFERENTIATE YOUR CLAIMS

Learn as much as you can about your competitors. Choose your claims depending on the prospect's top pain and the competition you are facing. Once you have a thorough knowledge of your market, you can actually choose your claims from a library of possible options and just do a copy and paste. When you prepare your presentation, choose only the Message Building Blocks that you may have prepared for a prospect with the exact same pain and the same competitive landscape.

If the pain and competitive situation between a previous prospect and this new one are different, you must redefine your claims. Remember, you must find or create something unique about your offering so you don't have to discount your price in order to be the most appealing. If you end up playing the pricing game with your prospect, it is because you skipped a step in the selling process and did not demonstrate enough gain.

STEP 3: DEMONSTRATE THE GAIN

Use only your strongest proofs of gain. Choose the proofs that are the most relevant to that particular prospect.

STEP 4: DELIVER IMPACT TO THE OLD BRAIN

Besides your proofs of gain, you should use a grabber (to create a strong first impression), a big picture (to create understanding), and powerful claims (to help the prospect remember your unique benefits).

Prepare to customize everything about your message around your prospect's specific pain. Sometimes a small amount of customization like copying and pasting their logo somewhere in your presentation can go a long way in giving them the feeling that you really are the only one who could cure their pain, and that your actions are totally dedicated to their benefit.

POWERFUL PRESENTATION POINTERS

Customize Your Message: If your corporate sales process provides you with canned sales presentations, take the time to revise them based on the Four Steps to maximize your selling effectiveness. Carefully construct your message for maximum impact to the old brain by using the Message Building Blocks. Do not underestimate the power of a grabber, good stories, and strong visuals. Reorganize your value proposition with proofs of gain so prospects can see the value without effort. Don't rely on your prospects to do the work: if you don't do the math of adding up the proven values of your three claims and subtracting your cost matrix, don't expect your prospects to.

Make It Short: Avoid any presentation that lasts longer than one hour. These types of events become "telling" events, not "selling" events.

Focus on Your Close: Repeat your claims one more time. Get some positive public feedback by asking: "What do you think?" Listen openly to their feedback; answer any objections they may have. Then let them commit to the next step: "What is the next step?"

If you thoroughly performed the Four Steps to increase your selling, the only outcome that makes sense for them is to buy from you.

Your Job Interviews

When interviewing for a new job, you are also selling a product: yourself. View the interviewers as you would any other prospects.

Step 1: Diagnose the Pain
Find out as much as you can about the job you are applying for. Why are they recruiting? What pain are they experiencing now without somebody in this position? For executive positions, help the company refine their diagnostic. They might think they need somebody with a certain skill set, when in fact you can prove that they need something entirely different; maybe they need somebody with *your* skill set.

Step 2: Differentiate Your Claims
Get a sense about the other candidates. Choose your claims accordingly. Listen to what skills the company is looking for, and listen carefully to what they say about you.

Step 3: Demonstrate the Gain
Prepare your proofs of gain: include specific statistics and concrete evidence of your past achievements. For example, "In five years under my management, sales at ABC grew 45 percent." Can you find a simple document that proves it? You will want to show your proofs of gain during the interview.

235

G

For Resumés: Include a testimonial by someone saying something relevant about you. This could include

- a reference list with recognizable names or companies.
- quotes of customers or past employers.
- recommendation letters, thank you notes, or appreciation letters.

STEP 4: DELIVER TO THE OLD BRAIN

Show the recruiter you are an expert at what you do—the perfect match for what they need. Be sure to deliver your message using the six stimuli: self-centered, tangible, contrast, visual, emotion, and beginning and end.

Summarize the three main skills needed in the position. Craft your claims around these most-needed skills. Demonstrate that you are unique with a prop, a story, or a mini-drama as appropriate.

In an interview, make strong eye contact and give a firm handshake. Use wording with "you." Don't talk about yourself; tell them what you can do for them.

In your resumé, change the order of things. For example, if you can get a quote from one of your previous managers, insert it at the beginning after your objectives.

Show your passion for the job and the industry. Make sure you have other job options so your fearlessness is real: nobody wants to hire a desperate candidate. For inspiration, you can reread the story about Agnes in the mini-drama section about grabbers.

RESOURCES

TITLE	AUTHOR	TOPIC
The Clue Train Manifesto	Locke, Levine, and Weinberger	E-commerce and Voice
Crossing the Chasm	Geoffrey Moore	Marketing, Strategy
Delivering Dynamic Presentations	Ralph Hillman	Presentation Skills
Descartes' Error	Antonio Damasio	Neurosciences
The Emotional Brain	Joseph LeDoux	Brain Research
Emotional Intelligence	Daniel Goleman	Brain and Intelligence
The Evolution of Consciousness	Robert Ornstein	Brain Research

Resources

TITLE	AUTHOR	TOPIC
Executive EQ	R. Cooper, A. Sawaf	Leadership
Fear Itself	Rush Dozier	Brain Research
How Customers Think	Gerald Zaltman	Marketing
How the Brain Works	Leslie Hart	Brain Research
Influencing with Integrity	Genie Laborde	NLP
Integrity Selling	Ron Willingham	Sales
The Leadership Challenge	James Kouzes	Leadership
Leadership in Paradoxical Age	Noel Tichy	Leadership
Leading Out Loud	Terry Pearce	Public Speaking
Loud and Clear	George Morrisey and Thomas Sechrest	Public Speaking, Presentation
The Magic of Rapport	Jerry Richardson	NLP
On Dialogue	David Bohm	Communication Theory
The One-Minute Manager	Ken Blanchard	Business, Management
Presentation	Daria Price Bowman	Presentation Skills
Presentation Plus	David People	Sales, Presentations
Presenting to Win	Jerry Weisman	Presentation Skills
The Primal Teen	Barbara Strauch	Neuroscience, Behavior
The Prospect Is King	Lee Harris	Prospect Service, Sales
Samurai Selling	C. Laughlin, K. Sage	Sales
In Search of Excellence	Tom Peters	Business
The 7 Habits of Highly Effective People	Stephen Covey	Business Efficiency

Resources

TITLE	AUTHOR	TOPIC
Strategic Selling	Miller and Heiman	Sales
Strategy Pure and Simple	Michel Robert	Marketing, Strategy
Synchronicity	Joseph Jaworski	Leadership
The 22 Immutable Laws of Marketing	Al Ries, Jack Trout	Marketing
Unleashing the Killer App	Larry Downes	Marketing
You've Got to Be Believed to Be Heard	Bert Decker	Presentation Skills, Brain Research

ACKNOWLEDGMENTS

We would like to address our sincere appreciation to Steve Hanselman, our agent, and to Kristen Parrish at Thomas Nelson publishing. Their pointed remarks have helped make this book more accessible.

We also would like to thank Bonnie Bright for her significant intellectual, design, and editorial contribution. Thanks also go to Frederic Neema of Frederic Neema Photography; Dave Gray of XPlane; David Becker, Philippe Becker, and Jay Cabalquinto of Philippe Becker Design; Benson Lee of DSignWright; Rick Crandall; Gail DaMert; and the many people who helped make this book a reality.

We also wish to thank the following companies for granting us the privilege of reproducing their advertisements: Air Canada, BMW, CareerBuilder, CarsDirect.com, DrugFreeAmerica.com, InFocus, IBM, Microsoft, NationWide, Office Depot, Smirnoff, and Sprint PCS.

ABOUT THE AUTHORS

Patrick Renvoisé, Co-Founder and President, SalesBrain

An expert in complex sales transactions, Renvoisé has closed over $2 billion worth of business. He managed global business development efforts first for Silicon Graphics, where he initiated, closed, and managed multimillion-dollar international OEM agreements. Then he served as executive director of business development and strategy at LinuxCare.

While selling supercomputers and complex software to organizations such as NASA, Shell, Boeing, Canon, BMW, Airbus, and more, Renvoisé met with some of the most brilliant minds on earth . . . and he became fascinated by the human brain. Using his engineering background, sales expertise, technology, and teaching experience, Renvoisé developed a completely new sales and marketing model based on the latest findings in neuroscience.

Passionate about teaching complex concepts in simple words, he has now dedicated his career to helping corporations better understand how their customers make buying decisions. Renvoisé grew up in France, where he received a masters degree in computer science.

CHRISTOPHE MORIN's passion is helping companies clearly identify what motivates and frustrates their prospects so that they can develop sustainable competitive strategies. Morin was CMO for rStar Networks, a company that develops private networks for Fortune 500 companies. Prior to that, he was VP of marketing and corporate training for Canned Foods, Inc., one of the largest grocery remarketers in the world. Morin has been interested in the workings of the brain for over twenty years, completing his masters thesis on the effectiveness of advertising in relation to hemispheric specialization. He graduated from ESC Nantes with a BA in marketing and received an MBA from Bowling Green State University. Morin is currently pursuing a PhD in Media Psychology at the Fielding Institute in Santa Barbara, California.

BOTH RENVOISÉ AND MORIN are recognized as pioneers in the new field of neuromarketing. In less than two years, they have become keynote speakers for many high-level marketing and sales events, and they have been consistently rated top expert speakers for Vistage, the world's largest CEO membership organization.

For information, please contact SalesBrain LLC at
info@salesbrain.net.